THE BARN OWL

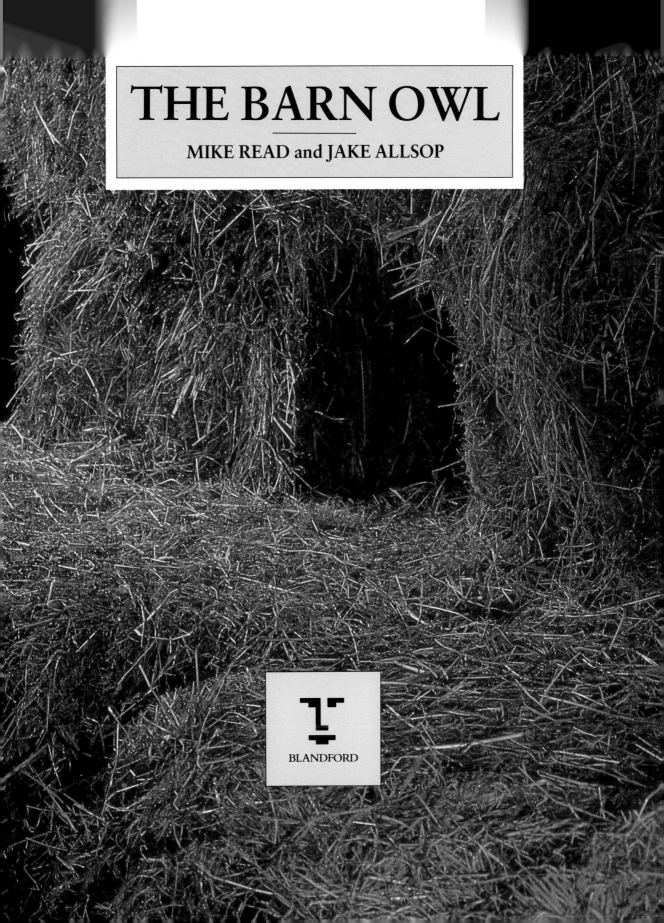

THE BARN OWL

MIKE READ and JAKE ALLSOP

BLANDFORD

A BLANDFORD BOOK

First published in the UK by Blandford
A Cassell Imprint
Cassell Plc, Villiers House,
41/47 Strand, London WC2N 5JE

Distributed in the United States by Sterling Publishing Co., Inc.,
387 Park Avenue South, New York, NY 10016–8810

Distributed in Australia by Capricorn Link (Australia) Pty Ltd
2/13 Carrington Road, Castle Hill, NSW 2154

British Library Cataloguing-in-Publication Data
A catalogue entry for this title is available from the British Library

ISBN 0-7137-2349-1

Typeset by Litho Link Ltd, Welshpool, Powys, Wales

Printed and bound in Hong Kong by Dah Hua Printing Co.

Contents

Acknowledgements

Among the landowners, farmers and gamekeepers who allowed access to their land, supplied information or helped in various other ways, we want to mention particularly Barbara Fairchild, David Fairchild, Dick Fenner, Peter Nix, Keith Sparrow and Don Whetstone in Cambridgeshire; Ray Dowe and Malcolm Rains in Norfolk; Keith Manley, Lord Manners, Mike Wiseman and Bob Wonham in Hampshire. We are grateful for information and help provided by, among others, Humphrey Crick and Dave Gibbons of the British Trust for Ornithology; Ian Johnson, conservation officer with the Bedfordshire and Cambridgeshire Wildlife Trust; Colin Shawyer of the Hawk and Owl Trust; and Bob Sheppard, the Trust's Barn Owl Conservation Network adviser in Lincolnshire.

Special thanks go to Chris Milsom, Bruce Berry and the staff at the New Forest Owl Sanctuary for the loan of birds, for advice, and for all the other help they gave; to Alan Revill and Judy Collins of the Upware Field Study Centre in Cambridgeshire for allowing us to share the experience of youngsters dissecting barn owl pellets; to Hampshire County Museum Service for the use of barn owl skulls for photography; and to Paul Brown for letting us have a copy of his report containing details of the Chittering barn.

Last but not least, we want to thank a number of friends: Paul Mason and John Morgan for reading the manuscript and suggesting many improvements; Mr and Mrs Henry Newland for allowing us to build an aviary on part of their land; Esther Richards for steering us safely through the minefield of the Welsh language; and David Crompton, Gerry Barrell and Martin King for helping in various ways.

Introduction

Nobody is indifferent to owls, least of all to barn owls. Owls provoke us into using adjectives we may not have much use for otherwise. We collected the following from a sample of people who were not particularly interested in birds: 'fascinating', 'spooky', 'majestic', 'creepy', 'ethereal', 'weird'. Note the emphasis on the two aspects of owls which strike people most: their dignity and their other-worldliness. This is what comes of having a human-like face, a capacity for remaining motionless and wise-looking for hours on end, and the doubtful habit of being out and about when respectable humans are all in bed. As to the noises which owls emit: they have voices which are capable of a range of outlandish calls and notes likely to make you jump out of your skin if you're not expecting them.

In fact, there are three species of owls you are likely to encounter in Britain without specifically being on the lookout for them. Perhaps the likeliest is the little owl, usually noticed as a motionless round ball of brown-grey speckled feathers surmounted by a ferocious expression. It is out and about during the day, often sitting on a fence post or a rooftop, or tucked against the bole of a tree. If you live where there are ivy-covered mature trees (a vicarage is as good a place as any), the one you are likeliest to *hear*, but least likely to *see*, is the tawny owl. It can offer you a fine repertoire of noises, depending on the time of year, from sharp ke-wick call notes (especially in summer when the young have fledged) to proper drawn-out hooting, characterized as mellow and musical by *aficionados* of the tawny owl, and as highly annoying by people who sleep with their bedroom windows open. During the day, what you are likely to hear is not the tawny owl itself (for it is quite properly asleep) but a clattering chorus of outraged blackbirds and other small birds mobbing it.

But the one you will never forget once you have seen or heard it is the barn owl. This is the species which calls forth all those adjectives, and more, because whatever qualities owls have in general, the barn owl has them all, in good measure. It is 'fascinating' we think, or we would not have written this book about it; and it is 'majestic', above all when it is quartering a field or hedgerow on silent wings in search of food. It is the quintessential bird of the twilight and the dark, ethereally white and ghostly in appearance, unholy in its eldritch shrieking, spooky (we could never agree to 'creepy') in its association with graveyards and church belfries. And 'weird'? Well, maybe it does strike some people as an odd bird, looking somehow top-heavy and knock-kneed, and having a somewhat mysterious lifestyle.

However, we, having studied it in all its moods, from gentle and playful to aggressive and quarrelsome, and having witnessed it in its many roles as lover, parent and hunter, have developed a great respect and admiration for it. It is, unfortunately, a bird under threat, so that our intention in writing this book is not only to share our experiences of and enthusiasm for the bird with you, but unashamedly to try to recruit you to the cause of barn owl conservation, to which we have devoted a separate chapter.

As with our previous book, *The Robin*, this is primarily a photographic study of the bird through various stages of its life cycle. Inevitably with the barn owl, as in our study of the robin, 'the focus shifts occasionally from the bird to the observers, a confirmation that our lives and the lives of the birds we studied became inextricably mixed'. Like the bird, we became crepuscular and slightly mysterious in our habits, lurking in the dark when good citizens were abed and frequenting out-of-the-way barns, derelict buildings and dead trees in remote copses. To all those whose lives were disturbed by our unholy activities in pursuit of the barn owl — to the farmers and landowners who tolerated our intrusions, and to the wives and soulmates who endured our neglect and our noisome odours — we dedicate this book.

The quotations at the beginning of each chapter are taken from a poem called 'The Barn Owl, a Plea for its Protection'. This was written around the beginning of the century by Mike's great great uncle, George Bentley Corbin, whose obituary appeared in *The Times* in 1914. The poem appeared in a locally published collection entitled *Stray Leaves from the Avon Valley, Hampshire*. The poem in its entirety is given on p. 124.

Note on classification
Classifications of organisms go from the general to the specific in a series of subdivisions. The most general category is the kingdom (e.g. animals, plants). Each kingdom is subdivided into categories called phyla, which are further divided into classes. Birds, for instance, belong to the phylum Vertebrata and the class Aves. In the class Aves

there are a number of orders (ending -formes). Owls belong to the order Strigiformes. Further division is into families (ending -idae); in the Strigiformes, there are two families, the Tytonidae and the Strigidae. Families are sometimes subdivided into subfamilies (ending -inae). The family Tytonidae has no subfamilies, but the family Strigidae has two: the Buboninae and the Striginae. Below this level of classification come the genera (the singular is genus) and then the species. The scientific name always consists of a generic name, e.g. *Tyto*, always written with a capital letter, and a specific name, e.g. *alba*, always written in lower case. Below the level of species sometimes come subspecies, designated by a further name, also written in lower case, e.g. *Tyto alba affinis*, often abbreviated to *T.a.affinis*. Table 1 shows how the most important European species of owl are classified.

Table 1: Classification of principal European owls

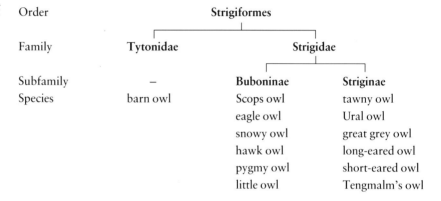

Order	Strigiformes		
Family	**Tytonidae**	**Strigidae**	
Subfamily	–	**Buboninae**	**Striginae**
Species	barn owl	Scops owl	tawny owl
		eagle owl	Ural owl
		snowy owl	great grey owl
		hawk owl	long-eared owl
		pygmy owl	short-eared owl
		little owl	Tengmalm's owl

1 Distribution

Beak set in a disk-like face,
Character of all the race.

Owls may be regarded as the counterparts of the diurnal birds of prey, although it would be more accurate to describe most owl species as crepuscular rather than nocturnal. Depending on whether you are a 'lumper' or a 'splitter', there are 120 or 140 species of owl in the world (The splitter strains to turn races and subspecies into species, while the lumper labours to do the opposite). This is half the number of diurnal birds of prey, about 270, or 290 if you include the vultures and the caracaras, no doubt reflecting the greater degree of specialization in owls, particularly their narrower range of feeding strategies.

These 120 to 140 species of owl are divided into two unequal families, the vast majority being in the Strigidae or true owls. The other family, to which the barn owl belongs, is the Tytonidae, a much more specialized group, with only 12 species in two genera: *Tyto*, which has 10 species including the barn owl, *Tyto alba*; and 2 species of bay owl in the genus *Phodilus* (The common bay owl occurs in tropical Asia; the African bay owl is known from a single specimen. Nothing more will be said in this book about bay owls).

All the *Tyto* owls bear a close family resemblance to each other, sharing the rounded to heart-shaped mask with surrounding darker ruff, dark eyes and long slender legs. They are similar in coloration, too, sharing a yellow-orange tinge to the plumage, but varying from lighter to darker. Albino (all-white) barn owls occur but they are very rare. A British breeder who has one is reputed to have refused an offer of £25,000 for it. We have seen pale barn owls, but never an albino, alas. The same is true of other *Tyto* species, alas again. Despite trips to southern Africa, where the grass owl, *Tyto capensis*, as its name suggests, lurks in the long grass, we have never seen this bird; nor, despite trips to Australia have we ever seen the lovely masked owl, *Tyto novaehollandiae*, or the truly spooky untinged sooty owl, *Tyto tenebricosa*. For more experience of these exotic relatives of the barn owl, the reader may well have to go where we have gone: to field guides and bird zoos.

Great grey owl perched on pine. This is a spectacular bird, with a facial expression which is at once fierce, thanks to its piercing yellow eyes, and comical, the concentric feathering making the eyes look too small for its face. It is as long as an eagle owl, the largest European owl, but not as bulky. Like the barn owl, it is quite slim under its loose feathering. It has a wingspan of one and a half metres, compared to the female eagle owl at nearly two metres and the barn owl at one metre. The great grey owl is primarily a woodland bird, inhabiting dense pine forests in boreal and arboreal latitudes from Siberia to Finland. Its range also extends to North America. Like the barn owl, it feeds extensively on voles, and in poor seasons will move southwards in search of food, but has never yet got down as far as the British Isles.

Table 2: *Tyto* species and their distribution

Scientific name	Vernacular name	Main distribution
Tyto soumagnei	Madagascar grass owl	Madagascar
Tyto alba	barn owl	world wide
Tyto rosenbergii	Celebes barn owl	Celebes
Tyto nigrobrunnea	Sula Island barn owl	Sula Island
Tyto inexspectata	Minahassa barn owl	northern Celebes
Tyto novaehollandiae	masked owl	Indonesia, Australia
Tyto aurantia	New Britain barn owl	New Britain
Tyto tenebricosa	sooty owl	New Guinea, Australia
Tyto capensis	grass owl	southern Africa
Tyto longimembris	eastern grass owl	India, Philippines, Australia

Hawk owl perched on pine. Its severe facial expression is very much determined by its splendid beetling 'eyebrows'. The hawk owl is about the size of a female sparrowhawk, with a wingspan of about 75 centimetres. It is thus intermediate between little owl at 55 centimetres and tawny owl at 1 metre. The bird, as its name suggests, is rather hawk-like in appearance, thanks to its longer tail, which helps it to be more agile in pursuit of prey and when hovering. It needs this kind of manoeuvrability, because, although its main prey items are voles, it depends on a diet of small birds in winter when mammalian prey is in short supply. Its range is similar to that of the great grey owl, but extends further south into Scandinavia, with the result that, in poor vole years, when it wanders further afield in search of food, it has occasionally reached Britain.

Tengmalm's owl perching on a dead birch. It is about the same size as a little owl, but with a large rectangular head, and a permanent expression of astonishment, thanks to its raised white eyebrows. It mainly inhabits northern taiga forests from Siberia to North America, but also occurs in Europe. In poor mammal years, when it is forced to wander outside its usual range in search of food, it occasionally gets as far as Britain. One curious feature of Tengmalm's owl in some parts of its range is its close association with the black woodpecker, whose holes it takes over for nesting. It has a plaintive but penetrating call, usually rendered as a series of po-po-po-po notes, which it utters continually throughout the night.

This is a widespread *Tyto* owl, the common grass owl, *Tyto capensis*. In Africa, it is peculiar to the southern half of the continent, extending north to the Cameroons and Kenya. It is similar in appearance to the African race of barn owl (they are both called *Isikhova* in Xhosa) but is somewhat larger, darker and longer legged. As its name suggests, it is a bird of open grassland. In some ways it is reminiscent of the short-eared owl, for it is a ground-nesting and largely ground-living owl. It is said to prey mainly on a veldt-dwelling vole, the vlei otomys, but is powerful enough to take larger prey. There is a lighter coloured version of the grass owl, found in India, China and Australasia, which some regard as a separate species, the eastern grass owl, *Tyto longimembris*. There is one other species of grass owl, the much smaller Madagascar grass owl, *Tyto soumagnei*, which is getting rarer and rarer as its forest habitat is destroyed.

The barn owl is by far the most widespread of the *Tyto* genus. In fact it has a wider distribution than any other species of land bird, owl or otherwise. As the accompanying map shows, it is to be found in every continent: Europe, from southern Sweden and south-western Russia to the Mediterranean; North and South America; many parts of Africa; India, Malaysia and south-east Asia; and Australia. Climatic and topographical overlays on the distribution map would reveal that it avoids mountainous regions like the Himalayas; cold areas like the northern tundra belt; severe desert conditions like the Sahara; and dense tropical forests such as the Congo. Otherwise, the barn owl is found in a wide variety of temperate habitats, in fact anywhere that is not too wet for hunting. We have to confess, though, that it has also eluded us on our African, Asian and Australian safaris, thereby denying us the desperately desirable thrill of seeing a familiar friend in unfamiliar surroundings.

Not surprisingly, with such a wide distribution, a large number of barn owl subspecies have been described, 35 according to some authorities. Of these, 22 are island subspecies, breeding in, for example, Madeira, Corsica, Sardinia, Cape Verde Is, and islands of the West Indies, Indonesia and Polynesia. There is even a subspecies, *Tyto alba punctatissima*, in the Galapagos Islands, where ten species of variant Darwin's finches caused the great man to ponder how such variation could lead to differentiation in species. The principal

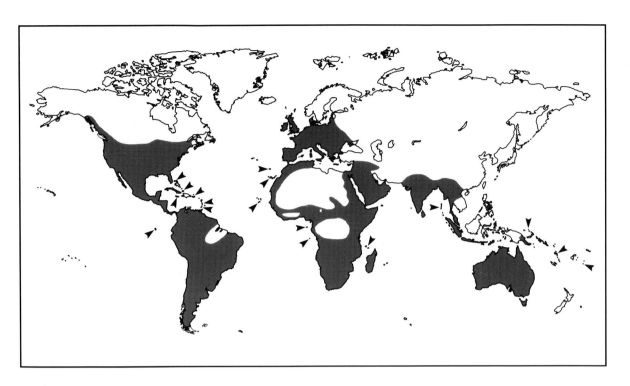

Figure 1: World
distribution of barn owl

subspecific variations of both mainland and island barn owls are in
their size, plumage and habits.

The smallest, *T.a. contempta*, is found in South America (it is also
the darkest race of barn owl), while the largest, *T.a.affinis*, from
tropical Africa earned notoriety when it was introduced into the
Seychelles in the 1950s. In this case, the barn owl's reputation as an
excellent mouser led to disaster. Rats being a problem in the sugar
plantations on the Seychelles, the powerful *affinis* barn owl was
introduced experimentally in 1951–2 to Mahe, where it quickly
established itself and spread. Food was plentiful. What nobody had
anticipated was that its preferred food would be the rare fairy tern, a
gentle and trusting colonial-nesting bird, which was therefore easy
prey. The barn owl left the rats alone, with the result that the fairy
tern population has been decimated, both owls and rats have
continued to thrive, and local people have benefited in that they can
now earn 30 rupees for every barn owl they kill. Despite this
cautionary tale, about 100 barn owls were introduced on to various
Hawaiian islands between 1959 and 1965, again to control rats on
sugar cane plantations. The American subspecies in question,
T.a.pratincola, is now established and its range is spreading.
Mercifully, there are no reports there that it has run amok as the
Seychelles barn owls have done. Not surprisingly, introductions,
even as biological controls, are now viewed with suspicion though,

fortunately, not all have been so disastrous. The little owl, introduced into various parts of England in the mid-nineteenth century,
was given a clean bill of health by the British Trust for Ornithology
in a survey of its feeding habits in the 1930s. Well, yes, it might take a
few game and poultry chicks now and again, but this is a small price
to pay for such an entertaining addition to our avifauna.

The palest race of barn owl is undoubtedly the British and south-
west Europe subspecies, the nominate race *T.a.alba*. Some writers
have compared this barn owl subspecies to a 'giant white moth', and
anyone glimpsing the bird in car headlights is bound to tell you they
have seen a 'white owl'. Witherby's *Handbook of British Birds*
(1943) calls it 'The white-breasted barn owl' and refers to it 'seen on
wing as ghostly whitish form at dusk'. To put this in perspective (it is
not in fact entirely white), compare this bird with its nearest subspecies, the race which occurs in north and east Europe, *T.a.guttata*,
which has substantial spotting on an orange-tinged breast and much
duller back and flight feathers. The *Handbook* is literal here, too,
calling the continental race the 'dark-breasted barn owl'.

All these island and mainland subspecies have arisen over long
periods in response to variations in local conditions. This, however,
fails to answer the fundamental question: why is the barn owl so

The dark-breasted Continental race of the barn owl, *Tyto alba guttata*, perched on a fencepost. It tends to be more spotted than our barn owl, the nominate race, *T.a.alba*. *T.a.alba* is the barn owl of western and southern Europe. The dark-breasted race, *guttata*, replaces it to the north and east of that range, but there is an overlapping area where the two races interbreed freely, resulting in considerable variation of plumage coloration and spotting on barn owls there. The dominant gene favours the darker colouring, which is therefore gradually spreading at the expense of the lighter. In years when a good breeding season is followed by a crash in prey numbers, birds of the *guttata* race occasionally reach eastern Britain.

Long-eared owl at a winter roosting site in a hawthorn hedge. The upright stance is typical of this owl, giving it an elongated appearance. It generally stands quite close to the trunk. Its stance and its cryptic coloration can make it difficult to see even in daylight, when this shot was taken. The ear tufts when erect give it a feline air, hence its dialect name, cat owl. The long-eared owl nests in trees, and takes readily to artificial basket nests, as at Woodwalton Fen in Cambridgeshire, which usually has a dozen breeding pairs. Elsewhere, it is widely but thinly distributed throughout Britain and Ireland. It breeds quite early in the year, starting like mistle thrushes and crossbills in February. It is at this time that you are most likely to locate a breeding pair by listening at night in suitable habitat for its quiet but penetrating hoo-hoo-hoo-hoo call. Later on, you might locate them by listening out for the young birds' call, aptly described as the 'creaky gate' call. In irruptive years, quite large numbers arrive in eastern parts of Britain from Scandinavia in the autumn, and can be found in roosts of several birds together. The specific part of its scientific name, *otus*, also means 'fool' in Greek, based on the belief that if you walk round and round a roosting long-eared owl, it will follow your movement, keeping its eye on you and turning its head until it wrings its own neck.

widespread in comparison to other *Tyto* species? We tend to think of the barn owl as a vulnerable species, declining in numbers and under threat from all sorts of directions. This may be so in the British Isles but the bird is a successful species in all other parts of its range. World-wide, it can tolerate a variety of habitats, as long as they are not wet or cold. It takes a range of prey according to what is available locally: one South American subspecies is recorded to have taken birds, bats and lizards, as well as local rodents. In the right situations, especially in the tropics, it will breed prolifically, sometimes having two broods a year, which is unusual for a bird of prey. It is tolerant of man's disturbance, too, and is often found near human habitation. Perhaps most important of all, it has few natural predators, so that, around the world, its numbers are controlled primarily by the mechanisms of food availability and, when weakened by lack of food, by disease.

Coming now to *T.a.alba*, we cannot paint such a rosy picture of the British barn owl. The barn owl is essentially a tropical species, and it is, quite frankly, pushing its luck trying to make a living in the uncertain British climate. It is very vulnerable to the cold and wet weather which often blights the spring and summer and reduces its ability to hunt and find prey. Similar considerations apply to passerine species like red-backed shrike, which is at the northern limit of its range, and now all but extinct in Britain. Breeding barn owls tend to be confined in Britain to lowland areas, predominantly farmland below 300 metres. Conversely, they avoid high altitudes such as parts of the Pennines and the mountains of Scotland and Wales. Those to be found in Scotland, mainly in the milder south-west region, together with a few hardy outliers in the highlands (Sutherland and Ross), are probably the most northerly breeding barn owls in the world.

If we compare the breeding distribution and density given in the 1976 edition of *The Atlas of Breeding Birds in Britain and Ireland* (Sharrock) with that given in the new edition, we can see that the barn owl's range and abundance would appear to have decreased, with especially dramatic reductions in north-west, central and south-west England, and in Ireland. The picture is, however, obscured by the fact that, for the first edition of the Atlas, a great deal of information about barn owls was provided by the public, and

The other 'eared' owl is the short-eared owl. This shot was taken at Pagham Harbour on the sort of marsh grassland where they spend the winter months. In such a habitat, and especially when it is, as here, perching on a fencepost scanning the landscape for prey, it is easy to identify. In flight, it is not so easy to separate from long-eared owl, since they are of similar size and coloration. As with other pairs of similar birds – common and arctic terns, glaucous and Iceland gulls, chiffchaff and willow warbler, and so on – different birdwatchers rely on different identification points. We favour the points given in *The Macmillan Guide to Field Identification* by Harris, Tucker and Vinicombe and well brought out in Alan Harris's accompanying illustrations: 'Short-eared owl [is] generally paler and sandier than long-eared owl . . . Note white trailing edge to wing [and] coarse blotching on upperparts . . . more solid dark primary tips . . . streaking mainly confined to upper breast.'

especially by farmers and landowners, in response to appeals on radio and in journals. This sort of appeal for public help was not made for the second edition.

We know, from our fieldwork in Hampshire and in the fenland areas of north Cambridgeshire, how many breeding barn owls we would have missed without the help of local landowners, game-keepers, farmers and farmworkers. The grapevine works like this: you go to a known site, check it out, and then go and chat to the farmer – call him David – and tell him what you have found. But you are never in a hurry. David likes to take his time to chat about the wildlife on his farm. Such a leisurely chat often produces some casual remark, like: 'By the way, my brother-in-law Keith used to have barn owls in an old bullock yard on his farm. I don't know if they're still there or not.' You prick up your ears at this, get an address and a telephone number, and off you go. In no time, having located Keith's birds, you chat to him, and he mentions casually that he saw a barn owl carrying food to a dead elm along a drove half a mile away.

Tawny owl at the entrance to a nestbox. Typical of a woodland owl, it has subdued, cryptic brown coloration. It is bigger than the barn owl with a wingspan well over a metre, and an average weight of 400 grams in contrast to the barn owl's 300 grams. Where the two species encounter each other, usually when the barn owl has selected a woodland edge for its nest site, the barn owl comes off worse. This photograph indicates the willingness of tawny owls to use artificial nest sites. This particular design is called the chimney box, and is slung at an angle below a branch. Just as barn owl boxes attract squatters like stock doves, jackdaws and kestrels, we have had all sort of other species in our tawny owl boxes, including stock doves, starlings and, unbelievably, great tits. The tawny owl is a widespread bird, found throughout Britain (but not in Ireland), and is catholic in its choice of nesting habitat, breeding everywhere from the old trees round a vicarage to a Highland forestry plantation. The tawny owl is the 'tu-whit-tu-whoo' owl, at least during the breeding season, and this accounts for its onomatopaoic Latin name *ululus*, which appears, via the Italian *allocco*, in its specific name *aluco*.

Who's the farmer? His name is John, and he turns out to be god-father to Keith's younger child. Off you go again, and the network extends until you can feel fairly sure that you have tracked down all the barn owls on your patch!

The problem with a public appeal such as was done for the Atlas, however, is, first, that the general public are more likely than farmers to mistake other owls, and especially tawny owls, for barn owls; and, secondly, that Atlas workers and organizers may not be as lucky as we are in having the time and resources to authenticate every report.

What then is the true number of breeding pairs in Britain? Earlier in the century one survey put the figure at 12,000 pairs. The 1976 Atlas estimate was 4,500–9,000 pairs. The wide discrepancy between upper and lower estimates is due to the difficulty of confirming breeding of birds, or indeed even finding the birds in the first place, given their unobtrusive nocturnal habits. For many records, the observer can only say that barn owls were present or that they possibly or probably bred. The observer cannot assume that the sight of a barn owl in the right habitat at the right time of year means that a pair actually bred, unless he or she found the nest, or saw adults carrying prey, or saw recently fledged young. Moreover, the breeding success of barn owls fluctuates considerably from year to year, influenced by such factors as weather conditions and the abundance of prey. This means that a survey in one year may give a higher or lower figure than in a succeeding year, making accurate statements about the bird's status very difficult. Since the 1976 survey, figures produced for the mid-1980s by the Hawk and Owl Trust suggest a continuing decline, with an estimated total of some 4,500 in Britain. On the other hand, an analysis of BTO nest records done by Steve Percival, and published in BTO Research Project 57, *Population trends in British Barn and Tawny Owls in relation to environmental change*, paints a brighter picture. Based on inform-ation from 1944, the start of the Nest Record Scheme, right up to 1988, the analysis showed that barn owl breeding success, defined as the number of chicks fledged per pair per breeding attempt, declined considerably in the mid-1960s and early 1970s but then improved substantially. Similarly, using ringing data for the years 1976–87, he was able to show that survival rates have been increasing since the mid-1970s. He concludes: 'Thus, for the country as a whole, the barn owl appears to be faring rather better in recent years in comparison with the 1970s; both breeding success and survival rate have been increasing over the period 1976–87, suggesting a population in a state of recovery rather than one of continuing decline.'

The 1993 Breeding Atlas, despite a reduction in the number of squares in which breeding was recorded from 1777 to 1110 between the two BTO surveys, concludes on a similarly optimistic note about

Little owl with young at a typical oak tree hole nest site at Ripley, Hampshire. Active during daylight and preferring farmland with hedgerows to woodland, it is more often seen than tawny owl or barn owl. Look out for it on fence posts and tree stumps roosting in hedgerows. It is often seen on the ground in pastureland since its main prey items, apart from insects, are earthworms and other invertebrates. It is quite common throughout England and Wales, with a population of 14,000 pairs (tawny owl is at least twice that figure). Its scientific name, *Athene noctua*, commemorates its close link with Pallas Athene, goddess of wisdom. It was known in the East Midlands as the 'Lilford owl', as, in the late nineteenth century, Lord Lilford imported Dutch little owls which became well established in Northamptonshire.

the status of the barn owl: 'Both breeding success and survival rates have increased on a national basis since the mid-1970s and there is good reason to hope that it may signal the beginning of a slow process of recovery.'

This improvement in breeding success can be attributed directly to the cessation of the use of organochlorine pesticides, like dieldrin, in agriculture, with a resulting decline in the levels of organochlorine residues in the corpses of barn owls and of other birds of prey, such as the sparrowhawk. The extent to which the British barn owl continues to lead a precarious existence can be attributed to the loss of suitable hunting and breeding habitat, a point which we develop in a later chapter.

As well as looking at breeding density, the BTO Atlas also provides information on the distribution of the barn owl in Britain. The distribution map given in Figure 2 shows that there are patches of the country where the barn owl is well established, such as the fenland area of East Anglia, but others where it is very thin on the ground, for example lowland areas in much of central England which on the face of it seem suitable. This may be to do with climatic conditions, but is also influenced by the fact that some parts of the country get much better reportage than others. Where organizations like the county Wildlife Trusts and regional branches of the Hawk and Owl Trust

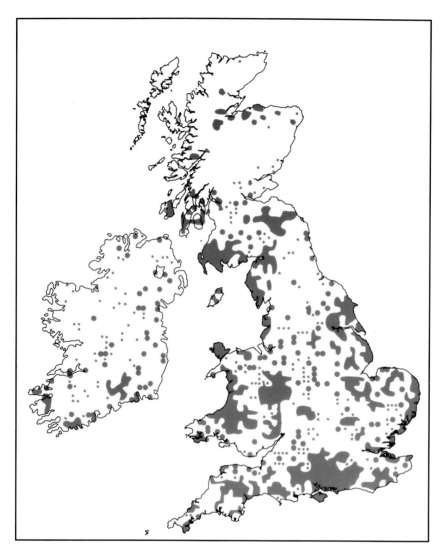

Figure 2: Map showing distribution of breeding barn owl in Britain and Ireland *(Source: BTO Atlas, 1993)*

are particularly active, and especially where they have extensive nestbox schemes, the coverage of breeding barn owls will be much better. Remoter areas may have birds that we just do not know about. For example, the 1976 Irish survey shows a concentration of breeding barn owls in County Kerry, explained, according to the Atlas authors, 'by the local Atlas organizer having many contacts in the farming community there'.

2 Description

Plumage soft as silkworm's spinning,
Fringèd wings and noiseless flight.

Typical plumage features of male and female barn owls. The male (left) is paler on the back and secondaries than the female (right). There are a few spots down the sides of his breast, but the female characteristically has much more speckling. There is much variation in coloration, so that the sex of barn owls is best determined by behaviour.

Among the visual delights of bird plumage, the rich tapestry of a barn owl's back feathers must count among the most beautiful. The truth is that wonderful patterns can be discerned on even the plainest bird. Think, for instance, of the wonderful vermiculations on the flanks of the gadwall, or the subtle coloration of the not-so-drab dunnock. The sheer richness and warmth of a barn owl's back does, however, take some beating. Shades of grey and of buff from yellow to rich reddish brown provide the background tones for a contrasting medley of alternating dark and light feather tips. When the richer shades predominate, the overall effect is to make the back appear darker.

This darker, greyer shade is particularly noticeable in female birds, although it cannot be taken on its own as a reliable indicator of sex. The tail and wing feathers have dark transverse bars, and these also tend to be darker in females. Similarly, a buffish tinge to the breast and spotting on the breast and flanks are more likely to occur in females. The fact is, though, that there is a great deal of variability in barn owl plumage. It is prudent to say no more than this: a generally darker looking bird is probably female. At the Church Barn nest, described in a later chapter, we could separate the female from the male on behaviour. She was remarkably pale, making the male seem considerably darker. At several other breeding sites, we were hard pressed to separate the parents, when we saw them away from the nest, that is, when there were no behavioural clues to go on. The great variability of barn owls' plumage had for us one great merit: it often enabled us to identify individual birds. Such a case was the Church Barn birds, where we could confidently say that the light bird was the female and the darker bird the male.

Allowing for these variations, it is reasonable to describe the barn owl as a pale bird. But why are barn owls so pale? By contrast, most other owls – tawny and long-eared owls, for instance – are quite subdued, cryptic even, in appearance, so that they merge invisibly into their surroundings. The snowy owl is no exception, since its whiteness, like that of the ptarmigan in winter, helps it to merge into the background. What is the advantage to the barn owl of being so visible? There is no easy answer to this question. Perhaps as a hole nester and a denizen of dark places, it has less need of cryptic coloration. Perhaps, for the same reason, it needs to be visible to its own kind, and especially to its offspring, which are themselves little more than balls of white fluff for the first weeks in the nest. On the darkest night, and in the deepest recesses of the nest, you can discern the chicks even without the aid of a torch. Similarly, you can make out the parent birds returning with prey for their young on the cloudiest starless night. If we can see them, then they can surely see each other. Some people object to this theory, citing the chestnut-brown oilbird, which spends its days in the deepest recesses of caves. It has been proved, though, that oilbirds find their way and each other by means of echo-location, similar to bats' radar.

If their pale coloration is a useful adaptation to the barn owls' lifestyle, it is trivial compared to the other amazingly sophisticated devices with which nature has equipped them. The combination of binocular vision and acute hearing, with the feather quality and the extraordinary aerodynamics of the bird, make it a more efficient flying and killing machine than, for all their electronic wizardry, any of the stealth bombers and fighter planes devised by man.

How well can barn owls see? They have binocular vision, a

The shape of the barn owl's face varies between round when the bird is alert, and heart-shaped when the bird is relaxed as in the next photograph. A closer examination reveals that the shape of the face plays an important part in the bird's role as a hunter of small mammalian prey. A flexible ruff made up of short, densely webbed feathers frames the face, turning it into a sound dish like a parabolic reflector. Notice, too, how the dish is split in two by the central ridge of bristly white feathers, a very striking feature when the head is seen in profile. We may assume that, when the bird is 'all ears' listening for the slightest sound of its prey, the ruff is positioned so as to make the sound dish maximally efficient, rather in the way that we cup our hands behind our ears to locate sound more accurately. The eyes themselves, being frontally positioned, are vulnerable to injury, and are therefore protected by a toughened nictitating membrane (a sort of inner eyelid, present in all birds).

A barn owl literally caught napping. The barn owl's facial ruff is in relaxed mode, and this alters the shape of the face quite noticeably. If disturbed, however, it may adopt a defensive stance: wings spread, head lowered, face forward, at which point the ruff becomes operational again, making the face appear as round and as formidable as possible.

characteristic of birds of prey which they share with primates. It is vital to species which hunt live prey, since it gives a three-dimensional view and thus tells the predator exactly where and how far away the prey is. Binocular vision works by combining two independent views of the same object. It is more efficient the further apart the eyes are, which is why many species of owls have flattened heads to get their eyes as far apart as possible. Measured in degrees, man's total range of vision is 180, of which 140 are three dimensional. The barn owl's total range of vision is 110, of which 70 are three dimensional, i.e. two thirds of its total field of view.

If you are the hunted rather than the hunter, your vision requirement is different: you want to have eyes in the back of your head! A good example of this is the woodcock, which, with its side-mounted eyes has virtually all-round vision without moving its head, but almost no binocular vision. But predators would also be at a disadvantage if they could only look ahead and not know what is going on around them. So, if your eyes are pointed forward, you need a compensating mechanism, and this is provided by the head-on-a-swivel principle. We can turn our heads through about 180 degrees at best, whereas the barn owl can manage almost full circle. A further trick in estimating the distance between yourself and your next meal is to make use of parallax, again getting two or more fixes on the same point. Many species of owl do this by bobbing up and down; little owls are a delight to watch in this respect. Although we have occasionally seen a barn owl 'bobbing', especially young ones in the nest, barn owls in our experience exploit parallax by swaying their heads from side to side rather than by vertical changes of position. Taken together, this combination of a pair of dark forward-facing eyes, a head that can apparently turn through a complete circle and the habit of sudden bursts of ducking and weaving makes owls at once beautiful and comical to behold.

The fact that owls have a relatively narrow field of vision can work to the photographer's advantage. If your barn owl settles one or two posts away from the one where you have set up and pointed your camera, you can, provided you do so quietly, move your lens on to your subject as soon as it looks away to the right or left. In other words, the movement you make will be momentarily out of the bird's line of sight. You could not, of course, get away with this trick with the majority of birds, as their eyes are side mounted, giving them the wide range of vision referred to earlier. We have also taken advantage of the barn owl's restricted field of view in other ways. For example, we were able, by standing absolutely still and, more importantly, absolutely silent, at the end of a fen dyke where a barn owl was hunting, to render ourselves invisible, so that the barn owl passed by apparently without seeing us. As this sort of thing happened to us on several occasions, we concluded that the barn owl was not as sharp eyed as legend states. One brusque movement or the slightest noise, though, and the game is up.

There is an old country belief that barn owls can see wonderfully well in the dark, but are more or less blind in daylight. There is no

This unlovely pair of pictures of a barn owl skull seen from both sides shows that the ear openings are at slightly different levels on the skull. This adaptation, and the fact that they are set at different angles, gives differential sound readings which enable the bird to pinpoint the location and distance of any sound.

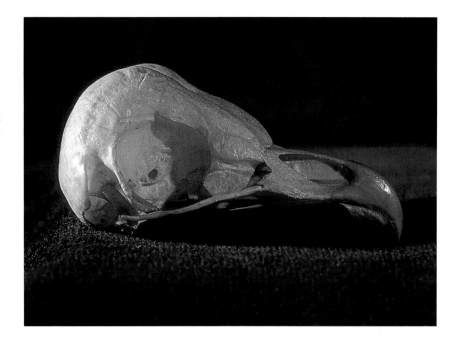

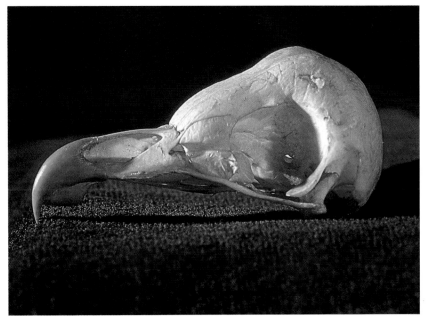

physiological basis for this legend, although it is true that barn owls have more night-sensitive photo-receptive cells (rods) than day-sensitive cells (cones). An American scientist, William Curtis, carried out some experiments in the 1950s to see how well barn owls could see in poor light. He did this by putting up perches in a closed barn between which the barn owls were made to fly. He then put up

obstacles in varying positions and with varying degrees of illumination on the obstacles to see how well the barn owls managed to avoid them. As he reduced the illumination down to virtual total darkness, the number of collisions increased. This demonstrated at least that the owls depended solely on vision to avoid objects. It also confirmed that their night vision is 50 to 100 times better than ours. That is to say, they make use of whatever light is available, however poor, and they can avoid colliding with unpredictable obstacles in conditions where we would be unable to move without bumping into things.

One important fact about the obstacles in Curtis's experiment is that they were noiseless, otherwise the owls would have been able to tolerate much poorer light conditions without collisions. For the truth of the matter is that it is hearing as much as vision that makes the barn owl such a successful night hunter. Put simply, the barn owl locates its prey by ear rather than by eye. It achieves this remarkable feat by virtue of two extraordinary features. First, its ear flaps are at

A female barn owl pouncing on a mouse. The photograph records the split second after impact. Her wings are still raised, but she will immediately lower them as she regains her balance and dispatches the mouse. In the split second before impact, the bird plunged, head forward with eyes fixed on the prey. At the last moment, she threw her head back, brought her fearsome talons forward into the line of fire, and went in for the kill. She has her eyes half-closed, maybe as an instinctive method of protecting them when catching prey in tall vegetation.

Barn owl primary feathers, the one on the right from a female, the one on the left from a male, with buzzard feather (top) for comparison. Primary feathers are the principal wing feathers used to achieve flight. Broad, square-ended wings, such as many birds of prey have, produce a lot of turbulence and drag, reducing flight efficiency. To compensate for this, some primary feathers may be emarginated (with the webbing narrowed down to the tip) so that the feathers are separated on the spread wing, creating a smooth airflow over the wing. This can be seen on the buzzard's feather. None of the barn owl's primaries are emarginated, presumably because it is not concerned with efficient flight at speed. Special adaptations of the barn owl's flight feathers, designed to achieve silent flight, are the velvety pile on the feather surface, and the extended barbs on the leading edge feathers which produces a sound-deadening comb-like fringe.

different levels on the head, are set at different angles and, most importantly, are movable so that the shape of the aperture can be modified, like rotating antennae to pinpoint the location of sound. Secondly, the barn owl's flat face with its flexible 'ruff' of bristle-like feathers acts as a sound reflector, pinpointing sounds with deadly accuracy. In addition, it takes advantage of a sort of binaural equivalent of binocular vision, making its fix from two slightly different readings. The analogy with the sophisticated target-locating equipment in modern military aircraft is again striking. Experiments carried out by another American scientist, Roger Payne, showed that in complete darkness barn owls would locate the position of a rustling mouse – he attached a leaf to it to simulate real-life conditions – before leaving their perch for the strike.

This aural acuity is not perceived as quite such a marvellous ability by the photographer in the hide. Note taking, for instance, becomes a real problem. A dictaphone is out of the question, but even the slight scratching sound of a pen on a page in a notebook causes the bird in the nest to prick up its ears. After a photographic session, Mike would often emerge drained, not because of normal fatigue or the lateness of the hour but on account of the strain of trying to remain absolutely silent for hours on end. This was particularly true at the early, sensitive stages of breeding, when he was after shots of courtship and mating behaviour, and knew that the slightest sound might put the birds off.

When hunting, the bird's use of hearing to locate prey is quite remarkable. Infra-red photography has confirmed that, in conditions when the bird could not possibly see its prey, it leads with its head, so to speak, to point to some rodent which is quietly, but not quietly enough, chewing on a piece of vegetation. The bird then flaps and hovers kestrel-like over its prey, head on target, legs dangling. At the last moment it brings its talons into the line of fire . . . and plunges to deadly effect.

If the barn owl can hear the rodent, why cannot the rodent hear the barn owl? People always comment on the barn owl's 'silent' flight, a characteristic which reinforces its reputation as a phantom. Here, too, the barn owl is magnificently equipped. The wing feathers have a wonderfully downy feel to them, thanks to a sort of velvety pile on the feather surface. This clearly helps to reduce the noise made by the bird in flight. In addition, the leading edges of the wing feathers have a fringe or fine comb which has the effect of deadening the sound the wing makes as it beats the air in flight. Stealth indeed, although the silence of its flight might have as much to do with the bird's need to listen out for the slightest sound made by its prey as with the need to sneak up undetected.

As the prey itself is not so active in broad daylight, the bird is adapted to hunting in crepuscular and nocturnal conditions, when most mice and voles come out to feed. We regard ourselves as a diurnal species, our activities commencing at sunrise and ceasing at sunset, and this is still the case where man has not extended his day into the hours of darkness by means of electric light. We therefore tend to regard nocturnal behaviour as something odd, sinister even, thereby adding to the poor old barn owl's spooky reputation, particularly since less than one in thirty of the world's bird species is in any sense nocturnal. (The ultimate nocturnal bird in terms of weirdness is the extremely rare kakapo of New Zealand: as well as being nocturnal, it is flightless and a ground-dwelling parrot – the surprise is not that it is rare, but that it should exist at all!) In contrast to most bird species, however, it is night time and the twilight hours of dawn and dusk when most mammals are active, so there is nothing mysterious about the nocturnality of the barn owl.

When we come to consider the aerodynamic design of the barn owl, we have to say that, if it were an aeroplane, it might well have crashed on its first take-off. Given its method of hunting, the barn owl needs to be able to fly at very low speeds, so that, unlike such high-speed killers as falcons, it has a very large wing area in relation to its body. Watching owls hunting, you can sometimes catch your breath as the bird slows to the point where it seems it will stall. It is as if it were only just managing to stay aloft. This is an illusion because, as bird ringers and other barn owl handlers will tell you, the bird is surprisingly slim under all that feathering. In other words, it compensates for its large wings by having a lightweight fuselage; if the body were any heavier, the hunting barn owl could easily stall and crash.

Barn owls can fly slowly, but can they fly fast? The image of the slow flapping is so ingrained in us that it comes as a surprise when one whips past you at the speed of a Mini on the inside lane of the M25. But the truth is that these barn owl 'burn-ups' are short bursts of speed, usually when returning to the nest with prey or when returning to the start of a hunting beat. The barn owl is not equipped for sustained fast flight, and this is confirmed by the bird's sedentary nature, although there is the occasional record of a ringed bird which has defied the experts by being recovered a long way from its point of origin. The current record, quoted by Chris Mead in his entertaining and informative book *Owls*, is of a bird which clocked up 1650 kilometres. Occasionally, too, continental barn owls of the race *guttata*, the dark-breasted form, turn up in Britain in the winter.

The majority of recoveries, however, involve young birds which have dispersed no more than 10–50 kilometres from their birthplace, and of older birds whose journeys rarely exceed 100 kilometres or so. The BTO's *1991 Ringing Report* quotes only three recoveries of barn owls (all ringed as nestlings) which are noteworthy because of the distance travelled: one from Devon to West Yorkshire at 359 kilometres; one from Cumbria to Cornwall at 464 kilometres; and a rare Continental recovery of a Netherlands bird recovered in Hull at 439 kilometres. To put this into perspective, in 1991, 1270 barn owls were ringed (1118 of them nestlings), and 162 were retrapped or recovered. In other words, out of 162, only 3 are noteworthy by virtue of the distance they travelled, the rest staying close to home.

This sedentary nature of the barn owl may well be related to its nocturnality. In his intriguing book *Birds by Night* Graham Martin

The barn owl's sharp talons show well in this shot. There is a sort of serration on the inner side of the middle claw which acts as a combing device when the owl is scratching its facial disk and rictal bristles. The outer toe and the hind toe are well articulated, so that the talons can be spread open in the form of a cross when pouncing on and gripping prey.

A barn owl using its beak to preen its wing feathers, making sure that each plume in each feather fits properly. To find out what is involved, pick up a flight feather some time and try doing the same thing! The serrated middle claw also comes in useful as a preening comb. One noticeable feature of barn owl preening is the amount of attention it gives to its leg feathers . . .

makes the point that 'knowledge both of the general characteristics of the environment and specific details of local topography are important for guiding an owl's behaviour under nocturnal conditions when visual clues are minimal'. In other words, the barn owl is much better off getting to know its local patch perfectly rather than straying further afield in search of good things.

. . . and to cleaning its claws, again using its beak. The claws constitute the bird's main weaponry, and must be kept in peak condition, in the same way that a soldier keeps his rifle clean and well oiled. While this photograph was being taken, the noise of the beak clicking as the claw was drawn through it was distinctly audible.

This shot shows a typical barn owl activity, scratching the facial disk and side of the head, paying a lot of attention to the ruff which plays an important part in the bird's hunting efficiency. The closed eyes might suggest mild ecstasy, but it is probably similar to the reflex which causes humans to screw up their eyes when sneezing.

We have concentrated in this chapter on the barn owl as hunting machine, suitably equipped for the purpose with fine senses and a well-designed body. Like all birds of prey whose livelihood depends on staying in peak condition, the barn owl looks after its equipment to maintain its efficiency. Feather preening is foremost among these. It is achieved by applying oil from the preen gland to the feathers using the beak as applicator. In their masterly study, *The Barn Owl*, Bunn, Warburton and Wilson noted how much attention the barn owl paid to preening the feet and the leg feathers. We noted the frequent use of the feet for scratching, especially the facial disk, no doubt because of the importance to the owl of this built-in parabolic reflector as a device for locating prey.

For this activity, the barn owl is equipped with a special gizmo, a serrated claw on the inner curve of the middle toe, which acts rather like a fine tooth comb. Allied to preening is a common barn owl activity which we call the 'feather shake', the sort of action performed by birds which have just bathed, but which is done by completely dry barn owls. Barn owls undoubtedly bathe, too, but it is very difficult to catch them at it. Mike had a pair of owls in an aviary which had a pond in the flight area. The owls paddled occasionally, but we never saw them indulging in the sort of shower-bathing with

A female barn owl ungallantly photographed early one morning, a time when she clearly did not look her best. It had been a very wet night, and she must have spent quite a lot of the night outside, out of choice not necessity, indulging in what may be called 'rain bathing'. Next morning, a routine inspection of the nest chamber through the peephole revealed the sorry sight of this bedraggled female, completely soaked, feathers looking as if she had put on wet-look styling gel. There was little change throughout the day, and more surprisingly no attempt at preening. In fact, it was not until late evening that she dried out and recovered her usual resplendence.

Female barn owl yawning, or more probably stretching her beak. The beak itself is weak compared to those of birds of prey like sparrowhawks, but it is well suited to tearing prey items into small strips to feed to its young. The adult often swallows its prey whole. The picture also shows the barbed tongue. (It is this barb, and the 'stickiness' of the roughened surface which answers the question about how on earth a blackbird can pull another worm out of the ground when its beak is already full.)

which small birds delight themselves and the owners of garden bird baths. Another incident is recorded in Mike's field notes: 'About 19.45, the female was on the main perch looking wet and bedraggled. Most of her body feathers were held out loosely to assist drying and her wings were held slightly open and slightly away from her body', which is reminiscent of the way cormorants spreadeagle their wings to dry them off. This particular bird got into a really filthy state as a result of the time she spent brooding her young in the nest chamber, and we began to revise our views about the purity of the 'white owl' of folklore. Then, one evening, we looked in to find her plumage restored to its pristine condition, as if she had been to a beauty parlour. The aviary pond was dry, so how had she done it? There was only one explanation: she had taken advantage of a rainy day to take an impromptu shower. We actually witnessed such an event. After a long dry spell, the heavens opened, but the aviary female, instead of taking cover from the downpour, raised her wings and gave herself a really thorough shower. Before we could think to point a camera at the scene, she gave a shake of her feathers and disappeared inside.

An interesting sidelight on the issue of barn owls bathing is the frequency with which they come to grief in cattle troughs. As it seems unlikely that they are trying to drink from the trough, for their prey items contain moisture enough, could they be attempting to bathe? Perhaps they are excited like Narcissus by their own reflections, but we are inclined to believe they come to grief while trying to splash water on to their plumage.

These descriptions of barn owls flying and hunting, preening and scratching, showering and bathing, might give an impression of a restless and active bird, but everyone who studies barn owls will tell you that what they mostly do is nothing at all. Maybe with their high energy protein diet, they need to spend relatively little time hunting. Be that as it may, the barn owl has perfected the art of inactivity: it can sit motionless for hours, while you, the dedicated observer, ache, literally and metaphorically, dying to shift your position or scratch your nose but unable to move for fear of disturbing the bird. When the bird finally does move, the event takes on cosmic significance. It blinks an eye or stretches a leg or shakes a wing before reverting to its catatonic state. You, the cramped and crippled observer, are so grateful: at last, an incident, something to record! Except that you cannot, for fear that the bird will hear the rustle of your notebook or the scratch of your pencil. Of course, the excitement and pleasure that we have gained from watching such activities as adults hunting, courting or feeding young make up for the frustrating hours we have spent waiting in vain for a roosting barn owl to do something – anything at all! This from Mike's field notes on a breeding pair suggests that even barn owls can become bored with barn owls:

> Male seems to have become something of a recluse. Female fairly relaxed. She often gave tremulous squeaky calls . . . She mostly got no reply from the male . . . He seems to spend most of his time 'seated' in the nest chamber.

Barn owls are also dedicated to conserving energy when it comes to vocal activity, being characterized as silent birds as owls go. They do in fact have a splendid repertoire of sounds and calls, some of them quite unbirdlike, including sounds described as screaming, purring, hissing, snoring, kissing, squeaking, chittering, clicking, snapping and sneezing! The call which the casual observer is most likely to hear is the unearthly scream or screech which has contributed so much to the barn owl's spooky reputation. A ghostly pale creature suddenly appears out of the darkness on silent wings, screams like a soul in agony and just as suddenly disappears again – this is the stuff that legends are made of.

The screech – 'a loud drawn out hissing scream with a marked gargling or tremulous effect (perhaps renderable as "shreeee")' to the ears of Bunn et al – is effectively a flight call, functioning variously as a territorial marker, a lovecall and a contact note. There are variations, some of them more like human screams, which are used when the bird feels threatened, and most likely to be heard by the casual observer who has accidentally strayed too close to the nest site.

The rest of the repertoire is mostly associated with in-nest activities: dialogues between male and female, and between parents and young. Some of the chirruping sounds between adults are tender and endearing, 'tremulous squeaking' being the most frequent description recorded in our field notes. Other notes of this kind are associated with begging for and offering food in courtship rituals. The young utter similar sounds when they are begging for food. Indeed, there seems to be an international avian language, differing little in quality from the begging calls of, for instance, the robins we were studying some years ago.

If you do stray too close to a barn owl nest containing young (we use the word 'stray' advisedly, as you need a special licence from English Nature to approach barn owl nests) you could be forgiven for thinking you have stumbled on a nest of snakes. Hissing, in addition to being a food begging call, is the owlet's way of trying to scare off intruders. It is similar to the note uttered by many other hole-nesting species, such as great tit and wryneck, and is characterized in the barn owl by its suddenness, its loudness and its persistence. You climb your ladder to check a nestbox, not knowing whether it contains young or not, and have to hold on tight if it does. Otherwise the vehemence with which they try to convince you that the box holds a nest of vipers could send you flying. And no amount of experience seems to diminish the effect on us of that first outburst of angry hissing.

3 Habitat and Territory

**Round the haystacks, o'er the meadows,
Stubble fields, and hedgerow sides . . .**

As we have already noted, the barn owl is a bird of the lowlands, preferring to avoid areas which are unduly wet or cold. Cramp, in *The Birds of the Western Palearctic*, summarizes its habitat requirement as 'mainly in open but not treeless lowlands, especially farmland with spinneys, hedges, ditches, ponds and banks, and some rough grass or herbage, roadside verges and similar rough terrain where mice and other prey can be hunted in low flight'. There is, as we know, a lot less of that sort of habitat in Britain than there used to be. It surprises some people to discover that the fenland basin of East Anglia is a stronghold of barn owls, given the area's reputation as a hedgeless, treeless prairie of barren monocultures. The fens have a number of features which are not apparent to the casual visitor,

Barn owl on a favourite fencepost. A typical barn owl hunting manoeuvre is 'post hopping', whereby the bird works its way along a stretch of roadside verge or field edge. Motorists observing a barn owl's plunge into the vegetation might think that the bird had injured itself, because of the way it seems to flounder. It is, in fact, 'mantling', that is, hiding its catch from the prying eyes of other predators.

A fen drainage ditch near Haddenham in Cambridgeshire. It shows a landscape characterized by intensive farming, but on each side of the drainage ditch there are lovely grassy banks that are the home of bank and short-tailed voles. These food corridors are vital to the barn owl's survival, and may account for its relative frequency in an otherwise barren environment. A lot of drainage ditches are being filled in and replaced by underground piped drainage. Fortunately, thanks to the efforts of bodies like the RSPB and the Hawk and Owl Trust, there is a much better understanding nowadays of their importance to wildlife, and most farmers and landowners are happy to keep their ditches and manage them sympathetically.

including a rich network of dykes, drains, ditches and drove verges which, for barn owls, are rather like long, thin supermarkets where they can hunt and find the protein they need. In addition, there are numerous oases, so to speak, in the fens, especially rough areas and spinneys set aside for game, and rough herbage and shrubs around derelict cottages and other abandoned buildings. We should add that the barn owl is not the only special bird in the fens. In addition to occasional breeding ruff and black-tailed godwit, most of the 30 or so pairs of golden oriole that breed in Britain are to be found in the fenland basin.

The barn owl is more closely associated with man and his buildings than other owls, and is happy around small groups of buildings, preferably without too much disturbance, where it can find the shady or dark corners it needs for its daytime roosts and for its nest sites. We have noticed that barn owls are quite prodigal in their use of space. For example, where nestboxes have been erected in neighbouring farm buildings and other suitable sites, a local pair of barn owls will use one box for roosting and the other for nesting. In successive years, the pair may reverse the use, so that we never know in advance whether last breeding season's occupied box will be used again this season.

This space requirement is equally true of the size of territory

occupied by a pair of barn owls. In a study of day-flying and individually recognizable barn owls (what good fortune!) in a young coniferous forest in Yorkshire, Bunn et al calculated an average territory size of 2.5 square kilometres. This, however, is rather small and reflects the rather specialized habitat in question. Given that, on typical farmland, the only useful feeding areas for barn owls are the narrow corridors provided by hedges, banks and ditches, and that these constitute a very small proportion of the total area of farmland, it is to be expected that a typical pair of barn owls will range over an area up to 5 square kilometres. One calculation suggests that a pair of barn owls may use 20 kilometres of 'food corridors' in a farmland territory of that size.

The population density in fact varies enormously depending on the availability of food and nest sites. In favourable habitat in lowland Scotland, a study showed that there was a maximum of 23 pairs in 50 square kilometres, i.e., just over 2.17 square kilometres per pair. In contrast, in upland areas in the same year, where there are probably fewer nest sites, there were only 11 pairs in 100 square kilometres, i.e., 9.1 square kilometres per pair.

The most thorough piece of research into barn owl territory that we know of is the RSPB study, 'Barn Owl Ecology on East Anglian Farmland', carried out by John Cayford. Using radio tracking, the researcher made a number of important findings. For example, the barn owl's winter range tends to be more extensive, some going 3–4 kilometres from their day roost to hunt. This is doubtless a reflection of the fact that food is harder to come by at that time of year. During the breeding season, on the other hand, the range shrinks, and most hunting takes place within a 2 kilometre radius of the nest site.

It is, of course, extremely difficult to measure accurately the territories of nocturnal birds without the aid of radio tracking. Our own observations are based on deductions from the number of contiguous pairs in the areas we have studied, and cannot be regarded as more than guesses. Indeed, guessing which barn owl is which when two or three pairs are under study in the same locality has become one of our favourite pastimes. It helps enormously when, as in the case of the Bunn et al study, you can distinguish individual birds on plumage details, idiosyncratic behaviour or flight patterns. One year, in one locality in Hampshire, our other main study area, there were two pairs nesting in natural sites – old trees – less than a kilometre apart. One of the nest sites was a regular and well-known one, but we were not at first aware of the existence of the other, so we had a great time trying to work out the extent of 'our' barn owls' territory. When we realized that we were dealing with two pairs, we could then identify which barn owl belonged to which nest site, but we never did determine the extent or boundaries of the territories of

An autumn hedgerow and drove near Martin in Hampshire. The rough grassland provides a lush habitat for hunting barn owls. In the winter, when mammalian prey is harder to come by, owls will sometimes try for other prey by 'buzzing' the hedgerow roosts of finches and other small birds.

each pair except for the invisible line which separated nest A from nest B. In other words, when one barn owl flew towards the territory of the other, we could make deductions about the territorial boundary, but when they flew away from each other, we had little or no idea where they went in search of food, or how far, apart from casual sightings as we drove to and from the locality.

Part of the problem is that it is rare to see any encounter between rival barn owls. BTO Breeding Bird Census workers are able to plot accurately the territories of most species of bird because of manifestations of rivalry at the boundary between neighbouring territories: singing, fighting, chasing, and so on. Barn owls in our experience rarely encounter each other in this way. To mark territory, we have noted how some birds will make a brief crepuscular tour of the immediate area round the roost/nest site, accompanied by the familiar screech call, or, more correctly, song, as its function in this case is to advertise ownership of the patch. In the aviary pair discussed in the next chapter, it was interesting that the birds, for the first week after being introduced to their new aviary home, were often heard uttering their 'loud hooty screech'. The notes taken at the time continue: '. . . no doubt due to the fact that they feel the need to establish territory even within the aviary'. As to encounters between rival birds, Bunn et al witnessed 'brief fights and angry chases by Barn Owls' in their study area, where, it should be remembered, the breeding density was unusually high. Mike's field notes for the two neighbouring Hampshire tree nesters (known respectively as Keith's and Oak) record a brief encounter between the males:

20.02: male leaves perch by Keith's nest and flies northward where it is met by Oak male. The two fly close and one (not known which, but probably Oak) screeched and Keith's flew off through the wood west, while Oak continued to hunt towards crossroads.

Once when in the hide at Keith's nest, Mike heard a fracas above him which he took to be part of a physical encounter between the Keith's and Oak males. On another occasion, Mike began to suspect that the proximity of the two nests was causing dangerous animosity:

29.6.92 Photographing at Keith's nest.

19.30	Into hide
19.40	Young commence calling
20.40	First visit by adult
20.58	Male takes in food
21.15	Male takes in food
21.20	Male takes in food

Only 2 further feeds between then and midnight when Liz came to get me out of the hide.

During the long absence of the adults (over an hour between feeds) after dark, I could hear loud barn owl calls from the direction of the Oak nest. Could there be some connection? Are the adults from Keith's giving some hassle to the fledging young at the Oak nest?

Another encounter in the breeding season is recorded:

At Fairchild's, 21.7.92, watching from viewpoint.

21.55   Unseen bird arrives (from general direction of Americas nest) calling, flies past beyond non-nesting barn and away towards hill still calling. Soon after more calls are heard and two owls are seen flying above the skyline, parallel to each other. The screech calling continues as they are lost from view.

Quite simply, where the territories are large and/or the breeding density is low, as is generally the case with birds of prey, boundary disputes are less likely to occur, and so the boundaries themselves take on a great elasticity. Intrusions go unnoticed, unless, as in the case of the Keith's and Oak nests, the distance between the epicentres is abnormally short. Cayford's RSPB study is quite specific in this matter:

In both summer and winter, home ranges of adjacent pairs overlap and there is no evidence that barn owls behave like other avian predators, such as kestrels, which establish exclusive territories in winter . . . The apparent lack of territoriality in barn owls may be explained by the fact that supplies of prey are variable and therefore difficult to defend; chance encounters are infrequent and depletion of prey negligible given the low densities of competitors.

A fascinating question about barn owls concerns site fidelity. In the north Cambridgeshire study area, we were fortunate in that local landowners and others kept us informed of their sightings of barn owls throughout the year, and not just in the breeding season when the birds are at their most vocal and most visible. The pattern which has emerged is that birds tend to leave the nest site after breeding, but have favoured roosts not too far away. As we have already noted, where alternative nestboxes are available, one is likely to be used for breeding and the other for roosting. This can be frustrating for Farmer A, who has barn owls in his box during the winter, anticipates that they will breed there, only to find that they have disappeared in the early spring. Conversely, his neighbour, Farmer B, begins to wonder why he put up a nestbox at all, for it remains empty throughout the winter until, miracle of miracles, a pair occupy it in spring and start to breed. We have not actually seen, but we can imagine, Farmer A's reaction when he is told the good news by Farmer B.

This sort of commuting between summer and winter residences is not confined to nestboxes. For example, in Jake's village, two barns less than a kilometre apart are respectively the breeding and roosting sites for a pair. To be more precise, we should say that one is the winter roosting site for the male. We are not sure where the female roosts, although we have flushed her once or twice from a nearby spinney. Once they pair up again, around the middle of February, both birds roost together at the nest site.

A good example of site fidelity occurred at a site near Sutton Gault at the foot of the Ouse Washes. A nestbox had been erected in a derelict house and used in successive seasons by a pair of barn owls. It was, in fact, twice vandalized and twice re-erected, and the birds showed remarkable resilience. Eventually the house was bought by a builder who decided to restore it. He was sympathetic to pleas about the barn owls and, before we could advise him on its location, had

nailed the box high in a tree in a small spinney some three hundred metres from the house. This was in early autumn. Next spring, the barn owls were happily nesting in it again, unperturbed by the house move!

All the above seems to imply that the same owls occupy the site in successive years. Bunn et al refer to sites occupied continuously for 20 or 30 years. They add 'there are several records, which seem reasonably acceptable, of up to seventy years'. There is merit in their doing so: it is a sure way of becoming totally familiar over a lifetime with the patch which has to supply all the birds' needs. The corollary of this is that, when changes occur which make the patch less attractive, the owls may be forced to move on. Evidence from ringing and field observation support the contention that individual barn owls remain generally faithful to their site, unless their barn falls down or their tree blows over, or, which is more likely, the habitat changes or the food supply disappears.

Nonetheless, we encountered one or two cases where a site was abandoned for no apparent reason after seasons of fidelity. This happened to the Fairchild's site (described in a later chapter) after a

Barn owl at sunset setting out on its nightly territorial flight, which is usually accompanied by shrieks to declare its presence. Later, it will go off to hunt along its regular field edge beat. Note how, even though no details can be seen on the bird, its silhouette – broad rounded wings and 'sawn-off' front end – is unmistakable.

spectacular series of seasons of large clutches and successful fledging. The nestbox was taken over by a pair of opportunistic stock doves. A box in the next barn which was traditionally used for roosting was our remaining hope, but it too was empty. We could detect no changes in the environment which could account for the disappearance of Fairchild's owls. The only major change, set-aside (land which had been taken out of production and deliberately left fallow), would presumably be a change for the good from an owl's point of view. So what had happened to them? We scoured the neighbouring fen, checking neighbouring sites which had been used previously only for roosting, poking into derelict sheds and buildings, asking everyone locally for news of barn owls. Nothing. True, the food supply that year was down, but not disastrously so, judging by brood size in other nests in the study area. True, some of the ringed pulli from previous years were recovered dead, but not in greater numbers than the national recovery average. If both adults had died during the winter, there should be other owls available, we thought, to move in from outside and occupy the site. The mystery had not been solved at the time of writing. (Note added at proof stage: the birds are back in breeding in the same nestbox after their year's sabbatical, but we still don't know where they disappeared to, or why.) In the meantime, the site owners are busy constructing and erecting more owl nestboxes: if their barn owls were ousted by squatters, at least there'll be accommodation available for everyone next year!

Barn owls seem also to remain faithful not only to their sites but also to each other, although, given the high mortality rate, there are regular changes of spouse. The fact that you come across two barn owls in the same roost (or two roosts very close together) outside the breeding season suggests that some pairs stay together throughout the year. How barn owls come together to set up house and breed is the subject of the next chapter.

4 Courtship and Nesting

**In the ivied ruin hoary,
Hollow trunk, or steeple grey . . .**

In books with titles like *Wonders of the Animal Kingdom*, there is bound to be a chapter on courtship rituals, those often elaborate ceremonies designed to attract and keep a mate and to facilitate mating and parental activities. Among birds, the strutting male peacock with his astounding tail, the Australian bowerbirds with their intricate seduction chambers, and the acrobatics of the brilliant orange cock-of-the-rock from South America come to mind. Thinking only of British birds, we recall the astonishing leks of ruff and black grouse, or the terpsichorean extravagances of the great crested grebe. We recorded in our book on the robin that even the most unassuming

Shot of a barn owl at a potential nest site out of season. It was taken, in fact, in winter. Barn owls tend to have two or three sites in the same locality, some of which they will use for roosting out of the breeding season. As the time for breeding approaches, the male tries to interest the female of his choice in one of them.

of birds have beautiful and often intricate rituals to form and reinforce the pair bond. The barn owl is no exception. Its courtship becomes evident as the spring equinox approaches. Then the male bird is more frequently abroad in daylight looking for delicacies with which to woo his mate or to entice a new one. Where a pair is formed, a beautiful flight ritual can often be seen – and heard, for it is somewhat noisy – as darkness approaches. It involves a sort of relentless chase of the female by the male, with one or both birds continually screech calling, giving the whole performance a frenetic quality. This is enhanced by the remarkable acrobatics in which they often indulge, twisting and turning as she leads him a merry dance. Occasionally, the female will settle on a perch to be wooed by subtler means as the male 'hangs in the air' in front of her in a fluttering display.

The male has another task to perform, namely to persuade the female to accept a nest site. This he does by a combination of stratagems, including enticing her to follow him into the nest hole, making little scrapes into the detritus on the floor of the chamber, and uttering persuasive churring calls. But the male does not make all the running. The female too has schemes to catch and keep her spouse, the most endearing of which is the ritual of courtship feeding. She trembles, begs like a baby owl and utters husky hisses (which some describe as 'snoring', a singularly inappropriate word, even though it approximates to the quality of the sound she makes). The successful outcome of all this ritual is mating and the onset of the breeding cycle. To reinforce the bond between them, the birds

An unusual nest site, a stack of beer crates on a Norfolk estate. The beer crates were originally acquired for transporting celery when the brewery, Bullards, went out of business. Although the crates were never actually used, the stack still stands. Jake can be seen apparently trying to see into the stack; his presence in the photograph gives an idea of the size of the stack. In the year when this was taken, kestrels took over the site, and the barn owls nested elsewhere. We found out about the site when the estate gamekeeper, Ray Dowe, told us how he had gone to the stack one evening to root out some foxes which he knew had their den under the stack. He sat in his vehicle and was amazed and delighted to see a barn owl fly into a cavity in the stack. For some time, he sat spellbound watching the owls carrying food into their nest. A little later on, the fox cubs emerged from their den to play. Eventually, a contented Ray turned his vehicle round and went home, his 12-bore still in its carrying case. This is, as far as we know, the only recorded instance of barn owls saving the lives of a family of foxes!

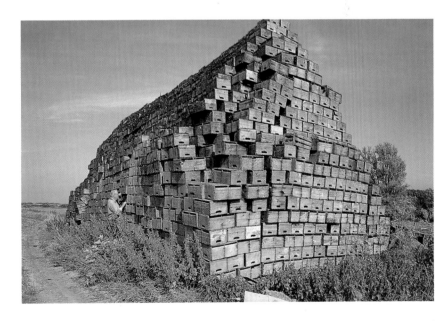

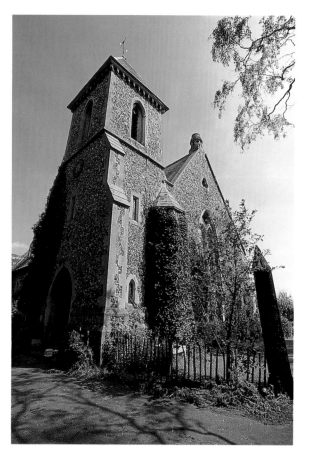

(Above left) The nest site most people associate with the barn owl, a church tower. This one is in what was a church but now a private dwelling. The owner takes a great interest in his avian squatters and seems not to mind the amazing mess of droppings and pellets which festoon the tower staircase.

Barn owls are regular in this tumbledown Elizabethan barn, with pellets galore to testify to their presence. In fact the front has fallen off the barn to reveal the interesting pattern of beams behind. The upper floor of the barn, which is no longer in use, has stacks of old bales, an ideal nesting site. Nearby farmland has been set aside, making the surrounding area a perfect hunting estate for barn owls.

Ruined cottages are not infrequent in the East Anglian landscape. They bear witness to the mechanization of agriculture and the consequent reduction in demand for the farm labourers whose homes these once were. This one is at West Row Fen in north Cambridgeshire, where our friend Gill Bangs keeps an eye on the barn owls that breed in it. The birds nest in a typical part of the house, namely between two joists above the ceiling. The cottage is in a dangerous state, but the local farmer recognizes that it is in effect a gigantic owl nestbox, and seems willing, thank goodness, to leave it to fall down of its own accord.

continue with their courtship rituals and acts of mating throughout the cycle, albeit at reduced frequency once the eggs are laid.

As to the preferred nest sites, as their name suggests, barn owls are fond of barns and other fairly dark and quiet farm outbuildings. Indeed farmers, to encourage barn owls in the days when mice and rats were a pest in grain barns, used to provide a special 'owl window', usually sited in the apex of the gable end, above the row of holes for doves. Barn owls' propensity to nest in church towers and belfries is also well known. Although we knew of a number of historical sites, we only came across one belfry nest in our study areas, at Little Ouse in Cambridgeshire. The decline of genuine 'moping owls in ivied towers' is probably due to our current craze for tidiness and, to be fair, a need to seal up towers in order to exclude less welcome guests such as jackdaws, starlings and pigeons. There was a time when barn owls themselves were regarded as a similar nuisance, as witness an eighteenth-century entry in a Norfolk parish church accounts: 'For worke and stuffe and nailes in stopping out ye owles at ye church, 3s 6d.'

In contrast to this hermetic sealing, when the new tower was constructed at Stickney Church in Lincolnshire, special access holes were provided for barn owls. When we visited the church, stock doves were sitting at the entrances.

Barn owls will sometimes make a home in very odd places. In a church the tower of which had been boarded up, enterprising owls got in by way of the outfall of the priest's toilet, and raised a brood in the pan. There is a report in *The Breeding Bird Atlas of Cheshire and Wirral*, an area where no more than ten pairs breed anyway, of a pair nesting in 1984 in a scrap car, no doubt driven to desperate measures by the lack of anything better. The pair which nested in the bell tower at Ravenscroft Hall, Middlewich in 1983 showed a greater sense of tradition. One of our friends, Malcolm Rains, who farms the fens near Downham Market in Norfolk, discovered a pair nesting in the chimney of his house, exploiting a ledge about three feet down. Unfortunately, jackdaws forced them to evacuate. Also in Norfolk, a gamekeeper put us on to a barn owl site in a stack of beer crates, which looks from a distance like a lonely Babylonian ziggurat in the middle of the fen.

We have been told of barn owls nesting on Ministry of Defence land on Salisbury Plain in boxes made from old artillery shell cases, including one bearing the legend 'Danger Bomb Simulator'. That ought to deter unauthorized intruders! A nestbox was also erected inside a Chieftain tank, which was eventually presented, complete with a decade of detritus and pellets, to the former Soviet government during the time of glasnost.

Apart from buildings, a traditional barn owl nest site is in haystacks and stacks of straw bales, whether inside barns or in the open. We have searched hard for barn owls nesting in such places, but found very few – only one out of thirty nest sites in the fenland study area. One possible explanation for the reduced use of this kind of site is the new European Community regulations designed to produce hygienic barn conditions which exclude not only germs but every other form of life. Another is the increasing use of modern balers which produce net-wrapped or plastic-wrapped circular bales. We have no evidence for our assertion that these are less attractive to barn owls than the traditional square ones, but the latter do seem to offer a better shaped and probably much less draughty cavity than the former. We accept, however, that barn owls can be very elusive in these stacks, tucking themselves away so well that their presence is often only revealed when, sadly, the nest is accidentally destroyed as bales are removed for use.

Despite the barn owl's lack of enthusiasm for woodland, more than a third of all barn owl nests in the United Kingdom are in trees, mostly in the boles of ageing or dead elm, oak or ash. The nest tree is invariably in a single belt along a lane or drove, or on the edge of a spinney or copse rather than in the middle. Of the two neighbouring tree sites photographed by Mike in Hampshire, one was a standard in a field hedgerow; the other was just within a spinney. The only exception to this rule which we found was at Wentworth in Cambridgeshire, where our friend Don Whetstone showed us a wonderful site: the remaining trunk of a solitary dead wych elm standing alone like a fire-tower in the middle of a long, narrow spinney. Don, lucky man, can sit in his garden in the evening and watch the barn owls returning with food to a nest site less than 200 metres away. It was Don who pointed out that his owls always carried their prey in the left foot. We checked and confirmed this. We have no theories about left-handedness in owls, and are open to suggestions. In a parallel fenland study of breeding golden orioles, we have noticed that about one nest in seven is left-handed, that is, it hangs in a fork to the left of the stem coming out from the trunk or main branch, suggesting that right-handedness is the norm among birds as well as humans. There must be a PhD in this for some enterprising student.

Barn owls do seem to choose romantic or dramatic settings as nest sites. The very isolation of the sites – remote or abandoned farm buildings or in gaunt dead trees – is itself somehow splendid and mysterious. The prose of our normally terse field notes becomes dangerously purple when describing, say, the moment we top the hill at Fairchild's, look out across Sutton Fen in the fading evening light and catch the first glimpse of our barn owl coming in with prey. When it comes to describing the nest itself, however, there is no need

Barn owls will not nest within woodland, but they will happily nest in the stumps or main branches of old, often ivy-covered trees on woodland edges and in hedgerows. Oak and elm are favourite, with ash, as this one is, a close third.

for noble adjectives. The nest is, frankly, not nice. The base consists of a sort of dry compost derived from the detritus of pellets. The adults will normally have been using the nest chamber for their courtship rituals since early in the year, with the male bringing in more prey items than ever get eaten. It is hard to say whether this excess is the result of over-zealous gallantry on his part, or an example of food caching against the time when food is hard to come by. Anyway, this excess prey accumulates together with the debris of regurgitated pellets to provide the untidy base for the nest chamber. When she is incubating, the female sometimes pulls pellets towards her to provide a layer for the eggs. It is a far cry from the neat cup nests of songbirds like the chaffinch or the song thrush. Also, unlike songbirds, barn owls are not particular about what happens to egg shells when the young hatch out. It is quite usual to find pieces of eggshell half-buried in the debris of a used nest, all adding to the compost. The young themselves may contribute to the nest by shuffling out a sort of hollow, often in one corner of the site, as they develop. In addition, prey items, which are at first torn up and fed to

51

the chicks until they are old enough to do it for themselves, are simply dropped whole into the nest chamber by the parents. In no time at all, a further quantity of decaying meat is added to the detritus. This is when the odours start to be really noisome. At the Church Barn nest, for example, penetrating wafts of ammonia caused Jake to gag and descend the ladder to recover his breath before venturing up to the nest again, handkerchief over nose, to check the young. To their credit, barn owls are careful about the removal of faecal sacs, until the young themselves are able to back to the edge of the nest chamber to defecate. The fact remains that an occupied nest site is not a place to linger. The young birds themselves can become badly soiled, with such encrustations on feet and feathering that it is sometimes difficult to believe that they will eventually turn into the immaculate free flying white owl of popular imagination.

In planning the photographing of barn owls, the most important sequences we wanted to get were courtship and mating. We realized that this aspect of the barn owls' lives would mainly involve at-the-nest photography at a time when disturbance to the birds was most likely to cause desertion. We realized, too, that the chances of finding a nest site occupied by wild birds which was suitable for the filming of this behaviour were slim. So, after much soul-searching, the

Mutual preening is one of the means by which bonds between animals are reinforced. The preening is mutual in that each bird in turn will preen the other. In this shot, it is pardonable to attribute human emotions like tenderness and affection to the birds' actions. The emotional tension is heightened by the chirrups of pleasure being uttered by the bird as it is preened. Observations suggest that in many pairs the female does more preening than the male, announcing her intention to do so with tremulous little calls to get the male into the mood. Chicks will also indulge in mutual preening, indicating that it has, like the mutual grooming activities of primates, a social as well as a sexual bonding function.

decision was taken to use captive birds, at least as an insurance in case no suitable wild nest could be found. Mike, who in a former life had trained as a carpenter, set about designing and building an aviary at the end of his neighbour's garden, having first checked that the other neighbours would tolerate barn owls and particularly barn owl noises around their roof-tops. Once the aviary, complete with nest chamber and flight, was ready, a pair of barn owls from the nearby New Forest Owl Sanctuary was introduced and invited to perform as amorous barn owls should. Of course they didn't. Photography is about an eye for a picture and the technical competence to capture it on film. It is also about faith, hope and a great deal of prayer.

Eventually, after exchanging the first pair of reluctant lovers for a more experienced and enthusiastic couple, Mike was finally able to record the behaviour we were after. Much of what follows is based upon observations of the aviary pair. Our primary reason for using captive birds was, as we have said already, to avoid causing harmful disturbance to a wild pair. The successful aviary birds settled down quickly and went through a complete breeding cycle without difficulty. We therefore have no reason to believe that the intimate behaviour we recorded is different from that of wild barn owls.

As noted earlier, courtship rituals which lead to successful pairing

Another bonding activity is courtship feeding, which in many cases continues well into the incubation period. Here, the male is feeding his mate at the nest. He does this in exactly the same way that she will later feed her young chicks, by tearing the prey item, in this case a vole, into strips which are then fed piece by piece. The whole ritual is reinforced by the food begging calls of the female.

do not cease once the serious business of raising a family is begun. Apart from mating itself, which continues during the breeding period, there are a number of activities which are, to our eyes, moments of great tenderness, including the continuation of courtship feeding. The female takes on the submissive, childlike role described above, and the male responds appropriately. Lest it be thought that there is sexist stereotyping in the last statement, we would add that the submissive–dominant relationship is more apparent than real. A note for 7 July (at the time, the male was temporarily incubating, itself an unusual occurrence):

10.45 pm: female brings in a vole which the male takes. F then resumes incubation. M tears up the vole and feeds it piecemeal to the female. There are frequent hiss-type food begging calls from the F when the M is less than attentive. Later, M collects a vole, which was also fed to the F.

The note concludes 'Much mutual preening takes place during this watch', a reference to another pair-bonding activity which, to our

This photograph shows barn owls mating. During courtship, copulation occurs many times during the night, and continues at a diminished rate during the entire breeding cycle. This photograph was taken at the nest site, where the female was already on eggs. Before the copulatory act, there is little or no foreplay. The female indicates her readiness by lowering her body. When the male mounts her, he holds the nape of her neck and uses outstretched wings to retain balance. The act is relatively prolonged, lasting as much as 20 seconds, in contrast to 3–5 second bursts of most other species.

eyes, seems to betoken affection and tenderness. It involves not only feather preening, but also what in doves is called 'billing and cooing'. In barn owls, the same activity is better described as 'billing and clicking', as they clash their beaks and click their tongues. They also have a most endearing way of rubbing their facial disks against each other, cheek to cheek as it were.

The most intimate moment and the most difficult to photograph was the mating of the birds. The balance between the needs of photography and the welfare of the birds is encapsulated in these notes for 13 May. The owls have settled in well, they have a clutch of four eggs. All is well. The decision is taken to try for shots of mating.

Morning
Set up the flash and lighting box ready for some photography this evening. Male owl leaves the box but female remains inside, incubating the four eggs.

Evening
Setting up started at 8.15 p.m., complete by 8.35 p.m. F nervous when I reveal lens and she leaves the box (M had already gone as I removed the peephole screw). When F returns about 20 minutes later, I allow her to settle before increasing the light level. With this increased light, I focus on her and then reduce the light levels again in the hope that the M will return.

After some time, F begins a very soft twittering call. M peeps into the nesting box and, despite some nervousness, he eventually walks in and mounts F, but they fail to mate and he leaves. I remain until well gone midnight. During this time, the owls mate four times, and I manage to photograph three of these. Each time, the F gives soft calls and also lowers head into a more inviting posture.

5 Egg Laying to Hatching

There he sits in solemn glory
Dozing through the livelong day . . .

The quotation at the head of this chapter certainly describes the female during the incubation of the clutch, when she works twenty-four-hour shifts with only occasional ten-minute sorties outside to perform necessary ablutions, preen, stretch and have something to eat, usually very little, often a morsel brought in earlier by her spouse. During these respites from duty, she often indulges in vigorous aerobics, described in Bunn et al as 'dashing about', presumably to keep in trim after a protracted period of squatting. The whole breeding period is quite long, a good 90–100 days, as is shown in Table 3, at the end of this chapter. In that table, and in what follows here, we are talking about what happens on average. It is important to bear in mind that considerable variations can occur, depending on such factors as weather conditions, availability of prey, the extent to which the adults are experienced hunters able to catch prey for their young, and so on.

The female lays her eggs at 2–3 day intervals. Barn owl eggs are unremarkable: white at first, until the nest detritus discolours them;

In the year when the Fairchild owls laid 10 eggs, of which 8 hatched out, the Hawk and Owl Trust in its Autumn 1992 issue of its newsletter, *The Peregrine*, reported an Avon pair which fledged 8 young, describing this as a record. The more usual clutch size is about 5. Fledging success is a function of such factors as weather and the availability of food, together with the continued survival of both parents. The *Peregrine* article noted that 'The youngest was almost the size of the eldest at the time they left the nestbox, which was unusual in view of the age difference.' This was also true of the Fairchild birds, and reflects the fact that 1992 was a good vole and mouse year.

matt, not glossy like those of stock doves, a bird which often competes with barn owls for occupancy of nestboxes; and elliptical, unlike the rounded eggs of other owls. They are small relative to the size of the bird, at about 40 × 32 millimetres. Clutch size varies between 4 and 6 eggs, although details have been published of clutches as small as 2 and as large as 11. Our record for clutch size was Fairchild's nest in 1992 which had 10 eggs, of which 8 hatched out. Even with an average sized clutch of, say 5 eggs, the interval between the first and last will be at least 10 days and often more. The problem with getting exact dates for egg laying, and subsequently an accurate figure for their incubation, is that this is precisely the period when disturbance by even the most careful observer may cause desertion. Moreover, some females will sit so tight that they will not leave the nest even with the observer peering into it. We had one report that there was an injured bird in a nestbox. The observer, who was licensed to inspect barn owl sites as part of a county nestbox scheme, had found the immobile bird in the box, and lifted her up only to find four eggs beneath her. He replaced the bird gently and retreated, reporting to us later the amazing fact that an injured bird, apparently unable to fly, was none the less continuing bravely to carry out her maternal duties. Careful watch on the nest at a later stage revealed that there were two adults and that they were both fit and uninjured. No doubt our colleague had come upon one of those stubborn females who would not be budged. All the same, desertion

Incubation is underway as the female settles on her clutch of four eggs. From a photographic point of view, this shot is spoiled by the small white insect just visible above the bird's head, but the scientific interest makes it worthy of inclusion. The insect is in fact a small moth, the larva of which is often found in the pellets and debris of barn owl nests. Indeed, if you collect pellets and leave them in a box for any length of time, you can be startled by moths flying up at you when you finally lift the lid. A frequently occurring moth in barn owl nests is a species of 'clothes moth', so keep your box of pellets well away from your wardrobe!

is always a possibility at this stage, and so we have preferred to leave our data incomplete rather than run this risk. For Fairchild's 1992, we managed to get these records showing progress towards hatching, waiting until the adults were away before approaching the nest:

16 July   1 chick and 9 eggs.
3 August   6 chicks, of which 1 very small.
               Unhatched eggs not visible.
11 August   8 chicks, of which 2 runts. 2 unhatched eggs.

The last two eggs never did hatch. Because the female begins incubating once the first egg is laid, there is a corresponding interval between the first- and last-born chicks, and hence a substantial difference in their size. This is well illustrated by Fairchild's chicks when we weighed them on 11 August:

Number	Wt in grams
Chick 1	325
Chick 2	280
Chick 3	275
Chick 4	250
Chick 5	240
Chick 6	175
Chick 7	125
Chick 8	50

Young owls always look endearingly cuddly. Tawny owl chicks usually leave the nest earlier than the stage reached by these young barn owls and look for all the world as though they are abandoned. Instincts to rescue young owls must be suppressed as they will rarely have been forsaken. Adult owls can rear them much better than can human foster parents.

By 25 August, chick 8 had disappeared, while chicks 1, 2 and 3 were already out of the nest and exploring their surroundings in the barn.

Because of the risk of desertion referred to earlier, our observations during laying and incubation were made on the aviary birds. Given that the primary objective in having a captive pair was also to photograph behaviour during this critical period, we were on tenterhooks as the pair went through their courtship rituals and occupation of the nest chamber, but with not an egg in sight. The situation was complicated by the regular presence on the aviary roof of a wild barn owl which would come most evenings and call persistently for a few minutes before moving on to try his luck elsewhere. This rogue had definitely set his cap at the female, and we feared that this intruder might spoil everything. To make things worse, the resident male was not very macho. To quote from the field notes for 20 March:

7.05 p.m.:   Wild owl present. Stayed there for some 5–8 minutes before flying off.

8.20 p.m.:   Wild owl back again.

10.55 p.m.:   Wild owl seen to arrive. Before its arrival, the male owl has been frequently wing spreading in threat display style, but once the wild owl was sitting quietly on the roof of the aviary, the male became much more retiring and eventually disappeared into the nesting chamber.

The female was, as the Victorians used to say, 'no better than she ought to be'. The field notes continue:

The female spent much time on the end perch just below the wild owl.

And, on a later occasion:

. . . wild owl returns and I hear very quiet calls between the birds, mostly a very quiet high-pitched wickering sort of call.

Finally, however, the couple managed to ignore the lurking Lothario on the roof. They settled down and a clutch of four eggs was laid. Although there are some records of males incubating, it is primarily the female's task, for which purpose she develops a large brood patch. The male, during this time, has light duties, principally bringing food to the female. Our male spent a lot of time in the nest chamber with the female, but observation of wild birds suggest that it is more usual for the male to roost away from the nest site, to pay no more than the minimum number of visits necessary to feed the female, and to look after the nest on the few occasions when she leaves it.

The female during incubation is, frankly, tedious to watch. You get positively ecstatic whenever she stretches, shuffles or changes her position – any action is as welcome to the observer as it presumably is to the sitting bird. Sometimes she will raise her body and turn the eggs, pushing them around with her face and bill. As the time for the first hatching draws near, the female shows increasing signs of restlessness, especially when the first chick starts to utter tiny cheeping calls from inside the egg. We missed the actual hatch which typically occurs in the morning, but the evening of 27 April brings wonderful news:

10-ish: Her drooping-wings style of sitting makes me check for a while. When she eventually moves, I am elated to see she has a chick beneath her!

By 29 April, the notes record that there were 2 eggs + 2 chicks. It is looking good for photography too:

> The female is relaxed and hardly reacts to any slight noises I make.

Next day, though, the news is not so good:

> One chick has disappeared from the nest today, there are 2 eggs and 1 chick. The female was feeding the chick, but I decided to take no photos.

By 4 May, the situation has stabilized. The field notes record jubilantly:

> Nest now has 3 chicks!

Photography is a problem, even though the birds have accepted any disturbance caused by the camera and its operator:

This barn-owl-in-jodhpurs portrait is in fact of the brooding female from the picture on p. 57. In order that her body heat can be transmitted directly to the eggs, she loses the insulating layer of feathering from her belly, creating what is called a brood patch. The gap in the feathering shows well in this photograph. In some passerine species, the incubation is shared by both birds, as evidenced by the brood patch which can be found on male blackcaps, sand martins, etc. In contrast, the male barn owl rarely incubates, but is committed to paying due attention to the female, keeping her company, bringing her food and making love as the opportunity arises.

No chance to photograph hatching as F keeps young fully covered.

During this period of the breeding cycle, with young to be fed and eggs still to be hatched, what we remember most vividly is the way the pair reinforce the bond that holds them together. Whenever the male visits in the nest chamber, the birds engage in vocal exchanges which to our ears seem soft and tender. The female utters husky notes, reminiscent of the food-begging calls of the chicks, as she greets her mate. The male makes gentle wickering sounds as he approaches her with food. There are intimate squeaky notes, too, to accompany their regular acts of copulation, perhaps the most powerful bonding of all.

Table 3: Timetable of events from first egg to young leaving the territory

Before hatch of first egg

31 days before	Laying of first egg
30 days before	Incubation begins
19 days before	Most clutches complete
1 day before	First chick calls from inside egg
0 day	First chick hatches
0 day + up to 14 days	Remaining chicks hatch

After hatch of first egg

Day 7	Young begin to vomit up indigestible matter, not casting pellets until older
Day 8	Eyes of young begin to open
Day 10	Young back out of nest to defecate
Day 11	Female now broods less closely and begins hunting for herself and young
Day 14	Young able to swallow prey whole
Day 15	Young intensely curious, exploring immediate surroundings of nest
Day 21 on	When oldest young is 3–4 weeks, female stops brooding, visits nest only to feed young
Days 35–42	Young exercise wings vigorously and make walking excursions from nest
	Occasionally older young will feed younger ones
Days 49–56	Oldest young leave nest
	Parents continue to feed young out of nest and remaining young in the nest until last chick has fledged
about Day 60	Fledglings start to play at pouncing on surrogate prey, e.g. pellets, flying insects
about Day 72	Fledglings start first serious swooping on prey from height
about Day 78	Any time after this date, young start roosting away from nest site and/or leave territory

6 Hatching to Fledging

But as darkness draweth near
This grand mouser has no peer.

As can be seen from Table 3, the breeding cycle of the barn owl is a prolonged business: at least 30 days from laying to hatching of first egg, and a good 60 days before all the young have truly fledged. This is the time when the mettle of 'this grand mouser' is really tested. The barn owl breeding timetable in Britain has been calculated from nest record cards submitted over the years to the BTO. Over 90 per cent of all nests become operational in the period April to June and, although there are records of first eggs being laid as early as February, the most frequent date for first eggs is between 21 April and 11 May. Projecting forward from this, we can see that the feeding of the young is in July and August, which is the period when mice and voles are most abundant. Our observation of other species, from blue tit to golden oriole, confirms that this timing of hatching to coincide with maximum availability of food is no accident, and that birds have the ability to predict variations in, for example, the hatch of their favourite caterpillar prey, and will bring forward or delay nesting accordingly.

The young of barn owls are altricial, which means they are blind, naked and helpless, and therefore totally dependent on their parents. Contrast this with the precocial young of, for example, waders, which are ready to get up and go within hours of hatching. The male barn owl is solely responsible at this stage for catching and bringing in items of prey. We never got tired of the sight of a barn owl coming in, carrying food in the claws of one foot, the prey invariably in line with the bird's body the way an osprey carries a fish. Before entering the nest site, the barn owl usually transfers prey to his beak. The left-handed Wentworth bird had a conveniently placed side branch on which he perched most photogenically to effect the transfer. The Fairchild's owl invariably paused on the window ledge to make the transfer before going up to the nestbox. Once he has arrived in the nest chamber, the male passes the prey item to the female. She tears it up into small pieces, which she feeds to the chick by straddling it from behind and dangling the food so that it touches the chick's bill or rictal bristles. The chick immediately homes in on the food item, opens wide and gulps it down. The aviary chicks provided us with

A sequence showing the growth of the chick, progressive replacement of downy plumage and development of the flight feathers at 1 day old, 3 weeks old, 6–7 weeks old, 9 weeks old and 11 weeks old.

similar observations, together with records of the characteristic calls of female and young:

> Whenever the young did not take the offered food, the female gave a chittering call to tell them food was available. They then begged – a hoarse squeaky call – and were fed. The female kept the young beneath her all the time, just raising her body a little to feed them. The two chicks appeared to be looking out from beneath her, the remaining egg between them.

Once she has a complete family of chicks, feeding becomes the dominant activity. How much the young get depends on conditions outside, of course, but it seems that from the mother's point of view there is no such thing as enough: she will continue to try to persuade her young to eat what father brings in, whether they want it or not. Bunn et al record the extraordinary case where, as they put it, 'one hen took 70 minutes to dispose of a single shrew!'

For the purposes of photography of the aviary pair, it was important that the prey items should be natural ones rather than the convenience food we had been feeding the adults on up to that point: dead day-old cockerel chicks. The aviary consists of an outside flight with food shelf, and an interior nest chamber contained within a shed for the photographer. The story of the weaning, and the accompanying frustrations, is revealed in Mike's notes:

> 2 May: 2 chicks + 1 egg in nest today.
>
> There were no cockerel chicks in the nest chamber this evening, so I decided to do some photography. Removed any cockerel chicks and replaced them with mice and voles on shelf and went into the shed to await delivery of food by the male. Waited for some time but, despite male being outside, he did not bring in any food. After a while, he brought in part of a cockerel chick, which was presumably on the ground outside. The female took this and commenced feeding the young. Prior to the male bringing in the cockerel chick I took three or four photos but was really waiting for him to bring in a rodent.

The tension begins to mount:

> After an hour of waiting, I went and checked the food shelf only to find that all seven or eight rodent prey items had been dropped on the ground. One vole has its head missing so presumably the male had realized this item was different from what he was used to and, not recognizing it as food, would not take it into the nest. I collected the mice and voles and cut them open a little, but still he

Female feeding very young chick. She stands in such a way that her body covers and protects it while she tears the food into small strips. In order to achieve this, she has gone down on her knees to cover the chick. She holds the prey in her foot to secure it, presses her wings down into the debris and uses them to push up as she rips pieces off the vole with her beak. As the youngster is still unable to see, she persuades it to eat by calling softly and by letting the morsel brush against its face and beak.

would not take them to the female. I eventually decided to place the usual cockerel chicks on the food shelf and he took four in ten minutes. Just my luck to have a barn owl that does not like mice and voles! He obviously needs some persuading . . . but how?

Ingenuity is called for . . .

3 May: I decided to try placing only mice on the food shelf. These included some white ones which I hoped would resemble their usual cockerel chick diet. The male still would not take them to the nest.

. . . and desperate measures . . .

As my need is to get the birds feeding on mice and voles, I waited untii the male went outside and then placed some mice inside the actual nest chamber. This was obviously going to be a big risk as I did not know what the female's reaction would be.

I was very cautious to ensure she did not see my face. To start with, I placed six mice in the nest. The female spread her wings and gave a very aggressive display at first, but at the same time she seemed inquisitive about the arrival of food.

65

. . . and holding of the breath . . .

Within five minutes, the female relaxed, picked up a mouse and started to feed her young. The male, no doubt having heard the feeding calls, arrived to investigate. The female would not release the mouse she had, so he picked up one of the other mice and took it outside. Eventually I placed more mice in the nest chamber. To be on the safe side, I also put two cockerel chicks on the food shelf and went to bed at 00.45.

The struggle continues next day:

4 May; 08.15: Many of the mice I put in the nest chamber were in the flight part of the aviary so I placed them in the nest once again. Presumably the male is removing them as the female is happily feeding on them.

But by evening there is some good news. . .

Nest now has 3 chicks!

. . . and some bad news:

No chance to photograph as female keeps young covered. Male is still being awkward about the mice as a food item. I'm not sure if he is eating any at all, but some have their heads missing. The female happily feeds herself and her young with mice. Thank goodness she doesn't need persuading too!

And the struggle continues, a battle of wits between stubborn male owl and stubborn photographer:

May 5; morning: most of last night's mice from the nest are now in the flight on the ground. Placed them inside the nest again.
  . . . and evening: placed mice in the nest chamber yet again as male refuses to take them from the food shelf. I have decided to feed the female, who will continue to feed the young on mice. I have not put cockerel chicks out for the male, in the hope that his eventual hunger will force him to change his diet.

And so it went on, neither party conceding, until 16 May, an occasion for lots of exclamation marks:

16 May: great day! Male is at long last taking mice into the nest chamber! Female leaves the nest and goes out for food too. This is

Because of the staggered egg laying and hatching, there is a corresponding difference in the size of the chicks in any brood. The second from the left is more interested in his surroundings than the others, who are more aware of the intrusive camera lens. Chicks react to an intruder in different ways. Some offer a threat display, lowering and swaying their heads, wings raised. Some start out like that and then bury their heads, ostrich-like, in the debris. Others throw themselves on to their backs and point their outstretched claws at the intruder. Our favourite is the 'possum' reaction, in which the owlet flops on to its back, closing its eyes and feigning sleep.

the first time I have seen her leave the young and go to collect food since they hatched.

Even now, though, there are frustrations for the photographer:

The largest chick swallowed a medium-sized mouse whole, but the female stood in the way so I could not photograph this.

As the young develop, the feeding pattern changes. At first the young get no roughage and so do not produce and regurgitate pellets of indigestible matter until after about two weeks, when they begin to swallow prey whole. From now on, the female joins in the hunt for food and no longer tears up the prey for the older chicks. The male continues to do what he has done from the beginning, which is simply to dump whole prey items in the nest chamber and leave the female, and later the young themselves, to cope. This is the time when chances of survival of the runts, the youngest chicks, becomes critical. If food is abundant, if the female has time to tend them, they

may survive. Otherwise, in the scramble for food the older and stronger siblings will take everything.

In checking nests during the growth of the chicks, our notes are full of references like 'runt has disappeared', 'no sign of youngest chick'. The conventional wisdom is that the older chicks are cannibals and will kill and eat their weaker siblings. Our own view on this is that most runts die naturally as a result of starvation or disease, and it is only at this point that they may become just another food item, and that only if no better food is available. After all, when the food supply is good, broods of five or six will reach the fledging stage. Even the prodigious Fairchild brood of eight produced six fledglings, while at Sparrow's site one year, a good vole year, three of the four fledged, after which the parents continued to feed the runt in the barn until it, too, was able to get away. In many cases when we had had to record 'runt has disappeared', a careful search of the barn floor revealed that it had fallen – or had been cast – out of the nest. In contrast to this somewhat ghoulish image of the big bad brother owl, the older siblings will often behave with great tenderness towards the younger, feeding them titbits – even when the youngster is full up and

Barn owl chicks soon become active and start to explore their immediate surroundings when they are about three weeks old. They constantly peer around, twisting their necks and swaying their heads from side to side to get a fix on whatever takes their fancy. Within another two weeks or so, the more adventurous will start to wander about outside the nest. In this picture, the one clambering up towards the entrance to the nest chamber is downier and therefore younger than the other chick, who is watching in awe its younger sibling's incredible act of daring. Within seconds of this shot, the older one also scrambled out of the nest on a similar voyage of exploration.

does not want to be fed! Bunn et al note that older chicks which feed the young in this way are invariably female.

When they are born, barn owl chicks, like the altricial young of so many bird species, are not pretty. Indeed they are positively reptilian, an aspect which their initial covering of dull greyish down does nothing to alter. But as they begin to acquire their second, pure white downy plumage, and later their flight feathers and facial disk, they become more endearing than any other chicks we can think of, including (dare we say it?) the robin. By the time they are three weeks old, they look like bundles of white fluff, a quilt to keep them warm now that the female has ceased to brood them regularly. The waxy sheaths from which their wing and tail feathers will emerge are not easy to see, and it is only when the young start experimentally stretching and flapping their wings that you become aware how much has been going on beneath the snowy down. The development of the familiar facial disk is more obvious and lends them their, well, *owlish* appearance.

They are fascinating not only in appearance but even more so in their behaviour, which tends to attract the adjective 'comical' as they try out the limbs and the senses with which nature has equipped them. Looking a little like the dotty myopic professor in a Rupert Bear story, they practise parallax, constantly bobbing and weaving their heads as if trying to make out some terribly important feature on the other side of the nest chamber. They experiment with their flexible necks, getting themselves into postures that would cause a circus contortionist to quit his job and take up hang-gliding. What makes it all so hilarious is that you have not one but a whole family of clowns to regale you with their tricks and pratfalls. For they also fall over, sometimes without warning, flopping on to their backs and closing their eyes, as if they suddenly felt the need for a nap. When they sense danger, they will all hiss, but the older ones will often lie on their backs, their sharp claws stretched out in front of them to keep the intruder at bay. Sometimes, faced with danger, the response, especially of the younger ones, can be exactly the opposite: they literally bury their heads in the nest debris, acting on the principle that if they cannot see it or hear it, it is not there. Similar behaviour can be noted in some shop assistants, politicians and bureaucrats if you present them with a problem they do not want to be bothered with.

In terms of entertainment value, a group of young owls is unbeatable, but we should remember that all this head weaving and wing flexing and falling over has a serious purpose: it is preparing them for the hard work of adult life which starts once they have fledged. This is when they must start to hunt for themselves, to learn to avoid danger and, in due course, to find a mate, nest and bring up

Young barn owls exploring the outside world. The one on the branch has very little downy feathering left, and will soon leave the nest altogether. He proved to be both adventurous and resourceful. While shuffling about on the branch, this one managed to overbalance and fall higgledy-piggledy down the tree, coming to rest on the trunk about five feet below the nest entrance. Undaunted, he scrambled back up, using his feet rather than his beak to grip, and flattening his wings against the trunk to get purchase.

As part of the warming-up process for the real world of flight, young birds wing stretch frequently.

young of their own. It is not easy to define fledging when it comes to young barn owls. When the nest is inside a protected area such as a barn, it is not unusual to find the young out of the nest when they are no more than 35 days old. During our first season at Fairchild's, we often found one or more of the older chicks on the floor of the barn or perched on a piece of machinery. At first, believing that they had fallen off the ledge of the nestbox, we would carefully gather them up and pop them back in the box. Eventually, with the experience of other young in other barns, we realized that it was part of their normal exploration of the environment. Mike occasionally had the weird experience, while photographing the adults bringing food to their barn-site nests, of having young flutter down and perch on top of his hide.

If we say that barn owls fledge at about 56 days, we mean only that they no longer regard the nest chamber as home, even though they might occasionally return to it at first to be fed. They do not stray from the nest site, however, and this is the time when you might be lucky enough to see three or four young lined up on a rafter in the barn or on a horizontal limb of the nest tree waiting to be fed. This is

also the time when it is easy to locate young barn owls because they are so noisy as they call and hiss to each other from various points around the nest site. They become more visible, too, as they start to play at pouncing on surrogate prey, such as pellets, leaves, flying beetles and other insects. They are not particularly graceful at first, but, in their determination, they soon improve. At first they play on the ground a lot, but as they increasingly take to the air they learn to avoid crash landings, and to score more direct hits. Finally, ten or eleven weeks after emerging from the egg, they start serious swooping on prey from a height. Once this stage is reached, the young leave or are encouraged by the parents to leave the nest site and find roosting and hunting sites of their own. This is the time when they are most vulnerable to the vagaries of the environment – being rained and blown on, being mobbed by other birds, and being mown down by fast-moving traffic – matters to which we shall return later.

Barn nesting sites often provide a secure and sheltered environment in which young owls can practise their first flights in relative safety. This individual, like its siblings, gradually increased its flying prowess over a few days before venturing into the world outside.

7 Food and Feeding Habits

Squeak or rustle in the straw
Met by an unerring claw!

In the Cambridgeshire area, the barn owls found abundant prey, especially wood mice, during the haycutting season. Luckily for them, this season is an extended one, some farmers cutting as early as the end of May, others not getting theirs done until well into August (We assumed the timing depended on some folk wisdom about the best time to cut hay; in fact, the late cutters are simply behind with their tasks!). At Fairchild's, the parents had an easy time feeding their young, because the adjacent field was mown at just the right time. Often the parent bird flew no more than 50 metres from the barn and dropped on a mouse or vole immediately. Thus, the frequency of feeding visits was high, about every three minutes. On the other hand, at a nest site with no newly mown field nearby, the time between feeding visits was on average 15–20 minutes; in poor weather, especially in wet and windy conditions, the interval could stretch to an hour or more.

On a balmy evening in early June at the Oak nest, the following visits were recorded:

20.07	M brings food to nest
20.09	M leaves nest
20.13	M brings food to nest
20.15	M leaves nest
20.18	M brings food to nest
20.19	M leaves nest
20.21	M brings food to nest

4 prey items in 14 minutes, or 3.5 minutes per item.

Conversely, on a cold evening later in the same month, at the nearby Keith's nest:

20.45	M visits with prey (s–t vole)
21.14	M visits with prey
21.38	M visits with prey
22.45	M visits with prey
23.10	M visits with prey

23.15   Left hide
5 prey items in 135 minutes, or 27 minutes per item.

Observation of birds returning to the nest with food together with the analysis of pellets enables us to say which are the barn owl's commonest prey items. Adult barn owls usually eject two pellets in every twenty-four hours, one in the evening and one in the morning. Chicks, which feed more frequently but with a smaller food intake at each feed, may eject more. In our study areas, the short-tailed vole (also known as the field vole) and the wood mouse (also known as the long-tailed field mouse) are the top of the list, although the proportion of each varied from year to year and also as each season progressed. Analysis of barn owl pellets reveals that barn owls will also take shrews and, occasionally, moles. Less frequently, and mainly in the winter when their favourite prey items are harder to come by, they will also go for birds like house sparrows and starlings, usually by the technique of disturbing them at roost and picking off the stragglers. They may even take the odd bat. Records of barn owls catching and eating invertebrates such as beetles relate to juvenile birds practising the arts of hunting on the nursery slopes, as it were, before trying for real prey. There are even records of barn owls taking young rabbits, but these must be regarded as rare occurrences. It was amusing for us that the pellet we dissected to provide the photograph on p. 79 contained a bird skull which we later identified as a robin, a bird we have devoted so much of our lives to in the past. In terms of percentages, estimates from various studies suggest the

A short-tailed vole, also known as field vole, is the barn owl's commonest prey item, often accounting for over half of its food intake during the breeding season. The life cycles of the two animals are closely linked: vole populations 'peak and crash' in a four-year cycle, with corresponding high and low barn owl fledging success rates.

following proportions of prey constitute the diet of the average British barn owl:

Table 4: Principal prey items

Prey	%	Consisting of
Voles	52	mostly short-tailed voles, some bank voles
Shrews	27	mostly common shrew
Mice	15	mostly wood mice, some brown rats
Birds	5	
Other	1	

Just as the snowy owl's fortunes go up and down in synchronization with the good and bad lemming years, barn owls will fare worse in years when the short-tailed vole population crashes. At such times, the increased proportion of shrews and mice in their diet may not be enough to compensate, especially when you think that the barn owl will need to catch two shrews for every vole in order to keep up the meat supply.

Most of us only see the smaller rodents when the cat brings them in or if we find them dead on a footpath. The different groups are not

A wood mouse, also known as long-tailed field mouse. Its long tail can be seen curving above it at the top of the picture. On average, wood mice constitute about 5 per cent of the barn owl's diet, although the percentage can be much higher in favourable circumstances, for example, immediately after haymaking. House mice and brown rats also figure in the barn owl's diet, especially around farm buildings during the winter months, when other rodents are much harder to come by. Remains of yellow-necked mice are occasionally found in pellets, too.

A bank vole, distinguished from the short-tailed vole by its reddish-brown colouring and its longer tail. A much less common prey, providing about 3–5 per cent of the barn owl's diet compared to the short-tailed vole at over 40 per cent, and the common shrew at 15–20 per cent.

A common shrew, easily identified by its long snout. A shrew's sensitive snout is constantly on the move, twitching and smelling out the terrain and the prey contained therein. Remains of the other shrew species – water and pygmy – are occasionally found in barn owl pellets too.

difficult to recognize. Voles can be separated from mice on their muzzles, their ears and their tails: voles have a rounded muzzle in contrast to the pointed muzzle of mice; their ears are small and partially buried, unlike the prominent and relatively large ears of mice; and their tails are shorter than their body, whereas the tails of mice are, or appear to be, longer than their bodies. Shrews are quite distinct, having a long, pointed snout, very small eyes, and their ears buried in their fur. It is harder, however, to separate the different species within each group. Most of the time, it was not difficult for us to identify, from photographs of the adults bringing in food, whether they were carrying voles or mice, but it was usually harder to be more specific. For mice, it is sometimes possible to separate the grey-brown of the house mouse from the purer brown of the wood mouse. The harvest mouse is, of course, quite distinct, being much smaller and having a lovely reddish-brown upper half contrasting sharply with its white undercarriage.

As to voles, the water vole (also known as the water rat) is substantially larger than the other two vole species. It has a body length of up to 20 centimetres. Its tail at about 10 centimetres is about 50 per cent of its body length, a proportion also found in the smaller bank vole (maximum body length 12 centimetres). The short-tailed vole is slightly larger than the bank vole (maximum body length 14 centimetres) but, as its name implies, its tail is proportionately shorter, at 30 per cent of its body length. On a quick view, the best identification pointers between the two smaller voles, apart from the tail length, are, first, the slightly larger ears of the bank vole,

Dissection of owl pellets being carried out by children at the Upware Field Studies Centre near Ely in Cambridgeshire in order to find out what the local barn owls had been eating. To dissect a pellet, it is best at least to dampen it. You can also soak it in water before breaking it up, still in the water, so that the fur will float to the top and the bones sink to the bottom. The children were able to separate the different elements: skulls, skull fragments, jawbones, ribs, leg bones, pelvic bones, shoulder blades and vertebrae. Apart from bones, some children were also able to retrieve identifiable strips of fur and feathers.

and, second, the chestnut back colour on adult bank voles. As short-tailed voles are much commoner in rough grassland than bank voles, it is not surprising that the former is the mainstay of the barn owl's diet.

What we know about the diet of barn owls comes not so much from field observations as from the dissection of pellets. What is a pellet? Owls swallow their prey whole. After digesting the flesh, the indigestible fur and bones are regurgitated as compact pellets. The characteristic barn owl pellet is large and fat, black and glossy, and easily separated from the small round pellet of the little owl or the slim brownish pellet of the kestrel, two species which will often roost and/or nest in the same sorts of buildings as barn owls. The only possible confusion is with fox droppings, but these, although black too, tend to be slimmer, and are always pointed at one end.

The dissection of owl pellets is a fascinating and absorbing business. At the Upware Field Studies Centre near Ely in Cambridgeshire, we were lucky enough to be present when a group of schoolchildren arrived from their five-mile nature walk clutching a plastic bag in which they had collected about 30 pellets from a barn where barn

owls were known to roost. The children knew what to do, thanks to a lively and informative pamphlet produced by Alan Revill, the warden at the Centre. The children began the dissection of their pellets at about three thirty, and it absorbed them to such an extent that they did not want to stop for five o'clock tea, something unheard of in the annals of young children! We were equally absorbed by the children's concentration and by the immense care they took to separate the different elements, and were able to confirm that voles and mice were the principal ingredient of the barn owl's diet. They also looked for, but predictably did not find, those tell-tale small, white scales which would indicate that the barn owl had been feeding on fish or reptiles.

Judy Collins, a teacher on secondment to the Centre and one of the most dynamic and interesting people we met during our study of barn owls, put two fascinating questions to us. First: what would you find in the pellets of barn owls from other parts of the world? Second: would it be possible for children from different countries to collect and exchange pellets with each other? As to the first question, what you would find in the pellet of, say, an African barn owl, the answer is likely to be: mainly rodents, but species unfamiliar to us like the giant Gambian rat and the cane rat. Elsewhere in the world there are records of local barn owls feeding on amphibians, bats and even fish, so the contents of their pellets could provide some wonderful surprises for the Upware children. Sadly, however, the exchange that Judy dreams about is unlikely to happen. The answer to the second question is that nature studies are virtually unknown in school systems outside the developed countries. Activities like the analysis of owl pellets, if they are carried out at all, are the preserve of university departments. Judy's idea of an international owl pellet school network is a beautiful one, though, and if anyone has any ideas how to achieve it, write to us and we'll pass the message on.

Back at the Upware centre, once all the remains had been separated, the children laid them out neatly on cards and labelled their exhibits. Specific identification was generally beyond them, but they had no problem in separating bird skulls from rodent skulls, and were able to distinguish the small flat skull of the shrew with its forward-pointing red-tipped teeth. Dentition, the arrangement of the teeth, is the way to separate species, and one or two of them managed at least to separate mice from voles, the latter's teeth having a characteristic zigzag pattern. We were touched and humbled by these children. These were town children, most of them unfamiliar with the countryside – one of them had even mistaken a horse for a cow earlier in the day – so it was wonderful to see how enthusiastically and skilfully they had taken to this work, and how much they had learned in such a short time about the eating habits of the barn owl.

Pellets of barn owl (top left), with pellets of tawny owl (top right), little owl (centre), short-eared owl (bottom left) and long-eared owl (bottom right) for comparison. Size, shape, colour, content and finding location distinguish the pellets of different species. Barn owl and tawny owl pellets are about the same size (5 centimetres long and about 2½ centimetres in diameter), but differ in other ways. The barn owl's is dark and shiny, smooth and solid; the tawny owl's is grey and furry to the touch. As their roosts are in different habitats, finding location is a good clue as well, especially with stale pellets. The little owl's pellet is smaller (about 2½ centimetres long and a bit over 2 centimetres in diameter, giving it a much more rounded shape). It is pale grey in colour, not compacted, so that it crumbles very easily. Insect chitin is usually visible. The pellets of the other two species are much harder to find. Short-eared's is barn owl size, grey in colour, soon fading and never shiny. Long-eared's is slightly smaller, similar in size and appearance to tawny owl's, but harder to the touch.

Of course we looked at pellet dissection as a means of learning more about the bird, but it is equally important as a technique for finding out about the incidence of small mammals in a given area. Much of the information we have about the distribution of rarer species such as water shrew and harvest mouse, for example, derives from analysis of owl pellets. The Mammal Society, in their useful leaflet by Yalden and Morris, *The Analysis of Owl Pellets*, also refer to the fact that the expanding distribution of bank voles in Ireland

This picture shows the contents of one dissected barn owl pellet. Skulls, sternum (breastbone), jaw bones, pelvic girdles, scapulae. In the bottom left-hand corner, there is a group of vertebrae. To the right and in the line above the vertebrae are ribs. In the bottom right-hand corner of the bones section is the beak of a robin. Other bones are leg bones. Down the right-hand side are the remains of fur and skin which formed the outer casing of the pellet.

has been monitored largely using owl pellets. For anyone thinking of trying pellet dissection, we would recommend three things: the Mammal Society's leaflets, which give detailed descriptions on dentition and other identification features; a lot of patience, especially when your carefully arranged display blows away in the slightest draught; and a good supply of paper tissues if, like us, you find you are allergic to pellet dust!

While we know *what* our barn owls eat, it is more difficult to estimate *how much* they eat. In his study, *The Identification of Remains in Owl Pellets*, Yalden used the information from pellet contents, bearing in mind that different prey items differ in weight, e.g., a short-tailed vole or a wood mouse is about 20 grams, whereas a brown rat or a mole is about 70 grams. He converted raw prey items into 'prey units' to take into account this weight difference, and it is calculated that a wild barn owl probably consumes about 120–150 grams of prey per day. We noticed that the aviary adults generally ate no more than two cockerel chicks per day, which represents about 80 grams, but we may assume that captive birds eat substantially less than wild ones as the former do not have to expend any energy to get their food. (There is, on the other hand, the phenomenon of caged birds which gorge themselves when the food is made available to them, a sort of comfort eating to counteract boredom.)

The weight of chicks is striking. At about mid-point in their growth, they weigh considerably more than their parents. The average weight of an adult ranges from about 330 grams for one in good condition to 270 grams for a brooding female. Of the brood of five at the Church Barn nest in 1993, there were two chicks at 370, one at 350 and one at 305 grams. Even the youngest weighed 240 grams. A lot of this juvenile weight is the equivalent of puppy fat. The weight of the young actually falls in the later stages as the fat is converted to muscle – muscle which they will need to face the hazards of adult life described in the next chapter.

8 Post-breeding Activity

Weird and white – among the shadows
Silently some creature glides . . .

When it is about 15 weeks old, the young owl can truly be said to have fledged in the sense that it has moved away from the nest site, learned to hunt its own prey, and has found its own roost site in a building or a tree. The act of departure is encouraged by the parent birds, who can even become quite aggressive to their offspring at this stage, regarding them as territorial intruders and wishing to see the back of them. At first, though, the young owl will not move far, perhaps no more than three to five kilometres from its birthplace. As they get older they tend to wander further afield. This is confirmed by the pattern of recoveries of young owls in the first year after ringing (which is usually done at six weeks old). In the case of the prodigious Fairchild brood, the first recovery was of a chick on the ground literally outside the barn door. From the state of it, we surmised that it had been nobbled by a fox. It was about 12 weeks old. The second recovery came about six weeks later, a road casualty picked up three kilometres away. The third was recovered about seven and a half months after ringing – 229 days to be exact. It had

```
                                                            GBT   GP26864
Species  BARN OWL                          SPV                       7350

Age Sex  NESTLING            BROOD 8         1

Ringing Information
         11  AUG   92  :            52 21'N      0  9'E
         HADDENHAM
         NEAR ELY
         CAMBRIDGESHIRE, ENGLAND                                     GBCA
Finding Information
         28  MAR   93  :            52 23'N      0  2'E
         HOLWOOD FARM
         SOMERSHAM
         CAMBRIDGESHIRE, ENGLAND          Finding Details            GBCA
Finder
         G LEONARD                         2 1-
         HOLWOOD FARM COTTAGES             FRESHLY DEAD
         CHATTERIS RD                      BIRD FOUND
         SOMERSHAM
         CAMBS PE17 3DW

                                    Distance   Direction    Duration
                                      9 KM    295 DEG      229 DAYS
RINGER
         J ALLSOP                                   Batch   2002
Ringer's Copy                                     310393   SYA   LPB
```

Figure 3: A ringing recovery form

81

travelled nine kilometres. The ringing details are supplied on a recovery form, a copy of which goes to the finder and a copy to the ringer.

As we saw in Chapter 2, most recoveries of barn owls ringed as pulli are well within 50 kilometres of the nest site, thus justifying their reputation as a sedentary species.

How well equipped is the young barn owl to deal with the hazards of existence? Physically, they should be fit when they leave the nest, after so many weeks of a solidly protein diet. They have moulted their body feathers into a more suitable plumage and their wing and tail feathers are fully grown so that it is no longer possible to distinguish them from adult birds. In terms of skill acquisition, they have, as we have seen, spent considerable time practising the art of hunting, chasing leaves and beetles before moving on to bigger game. They have learned to recognize danger – eventually – and should therefore have a good chance of survival.

Why is it, then, that so many don't make it? Bad weather, lack of

This picture reminds us of the high number of barn owls that meet their end on our roads, as many as 5,000 a year according to one calculation. The barn owl's low-level and leisurely flight makes it particularly vulnerable.

prey and disease will, of course, take their toll, as they do on all bird species. Lack of experience at hunting will put them at a disadvantage, too, compared to their elders and betters. They may occasionally fall foul of a predator, like the fox victim mentioned above, or may be unlucky enough to be set upon by another owl species, usually tawny owl. One summer, the Haddenham barn owls were exposed to an unexpected predator in the shape of an escaped eagle owl, whose presence was only disclosed when it swooped on Mrs Powers's dog (it missed). The reintroduction of eagle owls into parts of their range from which they had disappeared is a controversial matter precisely because it is such a killer of other owl species. Cases have also been recorded in the fens of barn owls being harassed by hen harriers. We also received a report from Hugh Miles, the noted wildlife camera-man, of a kestrel which, skua-like, robbed a barn owl of the prey it was carrying back to the nest. So persistent was the kestrel that only one of the barn owl chicks survived to fledging.

A related hazard, although rarely a fatal one, is mobbing by other bird species. Barn owls, because they tend to roost out of sight do not suffer the indignities of the roosting woodland tawny owls, whose daytime presence is often revealed by the cacophony of catcalls from chiding chaffinches and the like. When they are in flight, for instance when they are hunting, barn owls can become the victims of mobbing. We witnessed an interesting event of mobbing of one of the barn owls at a fenland site. Early one June evening, he was working his way low along his favourite dyke until he came to a spot where a hover seemed worthwhile. To our delight, a kestrel flew on to the scene and stopped to hover about ten metres above the barn owl. Were they looking at the same prey? Was the kestrel hoping to take advantage of the barn owl's superior weaponry? Or was it about to mob the owl? Before we could work this mystery out, enter two carrion crows stage left, bound for their roost, flying at about five metres, i.e., half-way between upper and lower bird of prey. Unlike Buridan's Ass, which, placed equidistant between two piles of hay, had no reason to choose one rather than the other and therefore starved to death, the crows had no hesitation: they harassed the owl, until he ceded defeat and flew to another spot. The crows, of course, pursued him, driving him further from his favoured hunting grounds until he and they disappeared from view.

Crows 1, barn owl 0.

In his book, *Adventures among Birds*, W.H. Hudson, an excellent but lately neglected writer on natural history matters, describes the converse of our crow experience. He has been keeping watch on a huge crow roost. For two evenings he had noticed sudden outbursts of unrest among the crows for which he could find no apparent cause. He describes what happened next:

On the third evening, the disturbance was more widespread and persistent than usual, until the birds could endure it no longer. The cawing storms had been breaking out at various spots over an area of many acres of wood, when at length, the whole vast concourse rose up and continued hovering and flying about for fifteen to twenty minutes, then settled once more on the topmost branches of the pines. Seen from the ridge on a level with the top of the wood, the birds presented a strange sight, perched in hundreds, sitting upright and motionless, looking intensely black on the black tree-tops against the pale evening sky. By-and-by, as I stood in a green drive in the midst of the roosting-place, a fresh tempest of alarm broke out at some distance and travelled towards me, causing the birds to rise; and suddenly the disturber appeared, gliding noise-lessly near the ground with many quick doublings among the boles – a barn owl, looking strangely white among the black trees! A little later, there was a general rising of the entire multitude with a great uproar; they were unable to stand the appearance of that mysterious bird-shaped white creature gliding about under their roosting-trees any longer. For a minute or two they hovered

Birds which die in this way are invariably face down, as this one is. Nobody is sure why barn owls are attracted, often fatally, to cattle troughs. In the summer, tragically many of the victims are breeding females, maybe desperate to bathe after being confined for so long to the nest chamber. Later, more young birds drown in troughs and water butts. What lures them to their watery grave is not clear. They may have gone there to drink or to bathe, or they may be attracted by their own reflection or provoked by what they believe to be a rival bird. Some may be after some morsel of food which they have seen in the water. The story of how this unusual photograph was taken is told in Chapter 12.

overhead, rising higher and higher in the darkening sky, then began streaming away over the wood to settle finally at another spot about half a mile away; and to that new roosting-place they returned on subsequent evenings.

Barn owl 1, crows 0.

To return to the prospects of our young barn owls, over and above what one might call the inevitable hazards, they do seem to be particularly accident-prone. If you consider the way in which birds die, as revealed by recoveries of ringed birds, you must conclude that their lack of experience of the world makes them very vulnerable to accidents like collisions with moving vehicles and with stationary objects like tree trunks, hitting or getting tangled in wires, or drowning in cattle troughs. These ways of dying are not peculiar to barn owls. A builder called us to deal with an owl which had drowned in an oildrum half filled with water. It turned out to be a young tawny owl. Barbara Fairchild rang us one October day to deal with an owl which had flown into her patio window. It was a young long-eared owl, mercifully only stunned. We have had cases, too, of

We have long become accustomed to road signs telling us about the possibility of deer, ponies or cattle wandering on to the road. This is the first barn owl sign to be erected in Britain. It was put up in 1992, and was designed by Avon County Council, in partnership with the Hawk and Owl Trust's South West Conservation Officer, Chris Sperring. It seems that the first evidence of the sign's success came two days after its erection, when a motorist phoned to say that he had just slowed down to see what the sign said when a barn owl suddenly flew in front of his car. He said that if he had not slowed down he would have hit the bird.

tawny owls strangled by fishing line, an accident which should happen less as fishermen respond to pleas to be more careful about tidying up after themselves.

All the same, there are accidents in which barn owls seem to specialize, above all collisions with fast-moving traffic and, occasionally, with trains. This is an inevitable consequence of their hunting style: predominantly low flight along road verges. In a Dutch study, quoted by Bunn et al, of 289 barn owls recovered in their first year, 103 were road casualties. No wonder that owl enthusiasts have started putting up road signs, like the one near Bristol, saying 'Caution: Owls in Flight', to persuade you that the best view of a barn owl is flying away from in front of your car rather than looking up at you from underneath it.

The decline in barn owls, along with many other birds of prey at the top of the food chain, has been partly attributed to secondary poisoning from organochlorines used as seed dressings. With the reduction or abandonment of this practice, there has been a notable recovery in the numbers of such birds, perhaps most marked in sparrowhawks, which are now common in East Anglia where they were near extinction in the 1960s and 1970s; and in peregrines, which have not merely recovered their numbers, but are reckoned to be more abundant than they were before the Second World War. Barn owls, too, have been doing well at least in certain areas of Britain. It is distressing, therefore, to learn from a study carried out by John Cayford for the RSPB, *Barn Owl Ecology on East Anglian Farmland*, that barn owls are once again vulnerable to secondary poisoning, this time from new kinds of highly toxic rodenticides which have replaced warfarin, to which rodents had become immune. In the winter, when field prey is difficult to find, barn owls are much more likely to hunt around farm buildings for rats and mice. Given that 90 per cent of farms in England use the new rodenticides, the danger is clear. Fortunately, one outcome of John Cayford's study is a campaign by the RSPB calling for tighter controls on rodenticide product labelling and application, together with exhortations to farmers to consider using less toxic compounds.

If you are a barn owl, the trick in this business of life and death is to get through the first year: after that, your chances of survival increase. The Southwest Lancashire Ringing Group's barn owl study, referred to in a later chapter, calculated from ringing recoveries that 65 per cent of these birds died in their first year, 17 per cent in their second year, 12 per cent in their third year, with only 6 per cent of birds living longer than three years. The British longevity record is 13 years. This record is of a ringed wild bird; barn owls in captivity can go on for much longer. Let us assume that one or two of Fairchild's brood of eight have survived, a reasonable estimate. They have

This barn owl in a frosty landscape is a reminder that many young birds are found dead during the winter months, a time when they are most in need of warming food and when food is hardest to come by. The barn owl is at the northern limit of its range in Britain.

avoided the many hazards we have described, and have beaten the winter with its additional threat of cold and wet weather. They are already capable of breeding, which is unusual as larger bird species are generally not sexually mature until their second or even third summer. The time has come to find a suitable nest site and announce it and yourself to a potential mate. We may expect, though, that young birds will not be very good at raising a family first time round. Just as most of the doomed blackbird nests you find in spring in shaky pyracanthas or on top of wobbly bicycle saddles are built by daft young birds, so the attempts of inexperienced barn owls at raising a family do not always meet with much success. From our limited observations, we feel that a more systematic study would reveal that many of the nests with scattered eggs or which produce only a single youngster in a good hunting season belong to first-year barn owls. Anyway, they mate, they breed, the young disperse, the parents retire to their winter roosts, and thus the cycle is repeated.

One important activity of the adult barn owl's year following the breeding season is the renewal of its feathering. Most bird species have a complete moult of their flight feathers in one go. Passerines have a progressive moult, whereby the feathers grow again in sequence, some new feathers being full grown while some old feathers remain, thus leaving the bird with reasonable powers of flight. Ducks, geese and swans, on the other hand, lose all their wing feathers simultaneously, rendering the birds flightless. Generally, birds of prey, because they depend for a living on their excellent powers of flight, are in continuous moult of their flight feathers, never lacking more than two or three at any one time. This is why you often see unsightly gaps in their wings and tail (and why some marsh harriers with missing central tail feathers get turned into black kites by the unwary). According to Ginn and Melville, the authors of the definitive book, called *Moult in Birds*, adult barn owls are in continuous moult throughout the year. Their primary moult starts in the middle of the wing with successive feathers on either side falling and being replaced. We cannot quarrel with this – knowing a little about barn owls is the equivalent of knowing a great deal about most other bird species – but support the observation of Bunn et al that a lot of the primary moult seems to take place in the summer: this is the time when an avid feather collector can find plenty of fallen flight feathers littering the floors of the buildings where the adult birds nest and roost. As to the moult of the secondary and tail feathers (retrices), we quote Ginn and Melville: 'S in 3 groups S1–S4 and S5–S7 ascendant, S12–S8 descendent; R irregular and slow', and are happy to leave it at that, seeing that we have no other choice.

In considering the factors which influence the life and threaten the success of the barn owl, we have so far said very little about the threats to their habitat and the conservation measures taken to counteract those threats. Colin Shawyer, director of the Hawk and Owl Trust and one of Britain's leading experts on barn owls, said: 'Barn owl conservation is about habitat conservation.' It is to these themes that we turn next.

9 Farming and Barn Owls

Eye and ear both wonder winning,
Hearing as acute as sight . . .

At the time when Corbin wrote his impassioned plea for the protection of the barn owl, the bird was heavily persecuted, along with all the other birds 'hooked in beak and claw', by gamekeepers who believed (some still do, alas) that they were a menace to their pheasants and their partridges as well as to their domestic fowl. On the other hand, most farmers had long recognized that the barn owl was a useful ally in the fight against vermin in barns where grain was stored. In the gable ends of old stone-built barns, you can still see, in the apex and above the row of holes leading to the pigeon loft, the 'owl window', an entrance specially made to encourage barn owls to stay and nest. Today, public expectations of food hygiene have never been higher, and environmental health regulations never stricter, so that a whole load of corn will be rejected at the least sign of contamination. But, even though strict hygiene has reduced the incidence of vermin, farmers still have to contend with rats and mice around their buildings. Unfortunately, today's remedy is not to

It would take more than the erection of a nestbox in this modern Dutch barn to make this place attractive to barn owls. The endless prairie of cultivated land is totally devoid of the sort of rough grassland 'food corridors' which the birds need for survival. The picture symbolizes the truth of the dictum that 'barn owl conservation is about habitat conservation'.

encourage barn owls but to open another pack of rodenticide.

Changes in farming practices and attitudes have, for good or ill, had a profound influence on the barn owl's fortunes. Let us begin with the bad news. Post-war farming has been characterized by the need to maximize productivity in agriculture. This has been achieved in arable farming spectacularly in the case of British farmers, by a combination of mechanization, the bringing under the plough of every available square metre of farmable land, and, as we have already seen, the intensification of crop production with the aid of fertilizers and an array of pesticides and herbicides. Mechanization equals bigger and bigger machines, which equals bigger and bigger fields, which equals the removal of hedges and the piping and covering of ditches, prime hunting habitats for barn owls where voles, mice and shrews are abundant. The deterioration of the barn owl's natural environment has been aggravated by the loss of much marginal land. In a nutshell, the problem is that the countryside has become too neat and tidy. All the nice rough bits, which naturalists treasure as wildlife havens get cleared away – think of a clump of thistles, a curse in a field of wheat but a boon to butterflies or a flock of goldfinches and linnets.

This atmospheric sunrise helps to show that farming and conservation can go together. The photograph was taken on the West Sedgemoor RSPB reserve, where cattle are used to manage the meadows. It is good for breeding waders, wintering waders and wildfowl, and, of course, for barn owls.

In the East Anglian fens, in particular, the encroachment of drove verges provides a telling example of the cleaning up of the country-side. Fen droves are effectively access tracks to and between fields. As their name suggests, they were often used in the past to drive cattle from one pasture to another. On the way, the cattle would graze the drove verges, which were usually wider than the track itself to enable carts to get round the ruts which soon developed during the wet season. Cattle grazing kept the vegetation down, to the benefit of adjacent arable farmers and of hunting barn owls. In the 1950s, as this practice diminished, the council roadman took on the task of keeping the rank vegetation down, but he, too, soon disappeared from the scene. Farmers whose land adjoined the drove took it upon themselves to keep the drove verges tidy, as they did not want weed beds next to their crops. What is the easiest and cheapest way of tidying up a drove verge? Run the rotavator over it; run a plough over it to clean the rust off the blades. Once that has been done, it is easy to see how drove verges became incorporated into adjoining fields. Drove verges have, in fact, been disappearing at an alarming rate. Feelings about drove encroachment run high. Some farmers have defended their incorporation of what is, in effect, public land into their property on the grounds that they are keeping down pests. On the other side of the argument, some conservationists have described drove encroachment as theft of public land. The controversy has thus generated much ill-feeling and much intemperate language on both sides.

While not condoning the many actions in the name of productivity and profit which have done so much to reduce the quality of the countryside, we feel that the continuing attacks on farmers by the conservationist lobby are not merely counterproductive; they are unfair. In our many dealings with farmers and landowners, we have been struck by a profound change of attitudes, especially among the younger generation. The majority of them are sensitive to their role as custodians of the countryside and its wildlife and are taking positive action, often at financial cost to themselves, to put matters right. Their work is supported by the farming press, which constantly emphasizes the need for the conservation implications of proposed courses of action to be taken into account. A good local example is the renewed interest of fenland farmers in planting poplars to replace the ageing stands which were an excellent cash crop in the days when timber was much in demand for the manufacture of matches. Poplar wood still has a market, though nothing like the guaranteed market of old. So, why are these farmers ready to consider planting poplars rather than, say, alder, which grow equally well in the damp fenland soil? Because they know that poplars (or at least certain strains of poplar) are the preferred breeding habitat of the golden oriole.

Current EC agricultural policy is also helping, particularly the policy of setaside whereby cereal farmers are required to take a percentage of their combinable land (i.e. where crops which can be combine harvested can be grown: cereals, pulses and oil seed rape) out of production to help reduce EC surpluses. We are less convinced that this is as beneficial as some conservationists believe. The regulations on compulsory mowing and ploughing ensure that the nests of thousands of ground nesting birds like skylarks will be destroyed. Locally, we became aware that we had breeding quail on setaside only after their nest disappeared under the plough. Vole and mouse populations are also badly affected, since cutting is done at the peak of their breeding season, thus reducing the food supply for barn owls. Farmers and government bodies are aware of these problems, and are making representations to Brussels to modify setaside regulations. So, has setaside benefited barn owls? The bird's preference, as we have seen, is for open areas of permanent unmanaged rank grassland, including field margins and drainage ditches. The problem with setaside is that under current regulations it is not permanent and is subject to continuing management while it lasts.

A view across Sutton Fen from the Fairchild's barn owl site which figures so much in our story. In the foreground is a favourite fencepost from which the birds could survey the stubble field beyond for likely prey. In fact they did not need to perch for long, as the field was alive with voles and mice following the harvesting of the cereal crop. In the middle distance is a derelict house, and further away in the middle of the fen, out of shot, another barn with a nestbox, both providing alternative nesting and roosting sites for the Fairchild birds.

92

The current EC requirement that a percentage of combinable farmland should be taken out of production has led to an increase in fallow headlands and crop field edges, which can only be good news for barn owls and other wildlife. Unfortunately, these setaside strips are unlikely to be permanent in most cases. On the other hand, an increasing number of farmers are sympathetic to the need to leave or to create wildlife havens on their land, and it may be that setaside will have pointed the way to an environmentally friendlier landscape.

Much more valuable is the encouragement to farmers and land-owners to create headlands to their fields, to tolerate rough corners and corridors on their land for the benefit of wildlife, and to leave, and where possible to restore, hedges, ponds and ditches. There are signs that this is happening increasingly, a reflection of the determin-ation of the sons to make up for the sins of the fathers, as it were.

We should, however, not be under any illusions. Rough land is always a potential nuisance to arable farmers. For example, in wet years, when diseases like rust develop more easily, they are much more noticeable on crops next to setaside and other land left fallow. Conservationists have long and rightly been vocal in calling on the farming community to take seriously its responsibilities as custodians of the countryside and its wildlife, but we believe it is equally important for conservationists to learn as much as they can about farming and about the constraints under which farmers work. In this way, it may be possible to have more fruitful dialogues and fewer intemperate confrontations.

After habitat loss, the problem for barn owls has been the loss of suitable breeding and roosting sites. Here, too, the passion for tidiness has led to the reduction of traditional barn owl havens, as old buildings have been pulled down, the trunks of dead elms and oaks have been uprooted, traditional barns have been replaced by functionally efficient but ornithologically useless ones. But here, too, the new generation of farmers and other landowners are taking steps to make good the loss, particularly with the erection of barn owl nestboxes. In Britain these may be provided by conservation

(Above) A female barn owl returning with prey to her nest in a traditional site: hay bales in a barn. The male is about to set off again on a hunting trip. The traditional bale stack or hayrick is a wonderful place to roost or nest, providing dry, warm and inaccessible tunnels between the bales.

Parent barn owl leaving the Church Barn. This shot presented particular photographic problems in view of the incompatibility of a black door and a pale bird. How it was achieved photographically is described in Chapter 12.

bodies like county Wildlife Trusts, the RSPB or the Hawk and Owl Trust, but just as often by the farmers themselves with no more prompting than an article in *Farmers' Weekly* on how to make a nestbox from a tea-chest and a plank of wood.

This chapter has dwelt on farming and barn owls, but it should be acknowledged that other bodies which hold large tracts of land are also making a contribution to barn owl conservation. Anglia Water, for instance, hold tracts of land along river valleys which are attractive habitat for barn owls, lacking only nesting sites to make them irresistible. Thanks to the Hawk and Owl Trust, sewage works and pumping stations belonging to Anglia Water are now adorned with barn owl nestboxes, with encouraging signs that they are being used. It is this kind of conservation initiative which will be discussed next.

10 Barn Owls and Conservation

Game-preserver, farmer, all
Might him Benefactor call.

Rarely can a single species of bird have been the subject of such a broad-based conservation effort as the barn owl. In Britain every national and local body involved with natural history matters is likely to have some involvement, from the conducting of scientific surveys and the publication of information leaflets to nestbox schemes and schools-based projects. For national bird organizations like the BTO and the RSPB, the barn owl is just one of a number of threatened species which they have to be concerned with. The work of the two organizations overlaps, but there are differences. The BTO's primary concern is to gather accurate information about the current and changing status and the requirements of species like the barn owl, the stone curlew and the woodlark, in order that decisions will be as well informed as possible. The RSPB, while carrying out dedicated studies on species, puts a lot of its effort into the protection of the species, through management of habitat, publicity persuasion campaigns and educational initiatives.

The RSPB's East Anglian Survey, referred to in an earlier chapter, has made an invaluable contribution to our knowledge of the barn owl's requirements, providing solid scientific information. It contains much practical information, as for instance the section on habitat, written in a refreshingly direct, imperative style:

Retain grass edges to fields, especially along hedges and beside ditches, rivers, streams, etc – a strip of three to five metres wide is best. Similarly, grass strips along wood edges should be as wide as possible (at least three to five metres). Provide or retain fence posts as hunting perches. Do not cut grass too closely, too frequently or more than is required for access; retain long grass at the sides and tussocks, etc. as cover for voles.

Its 'How you can help' section is equally to the point:

Leave well alone! Existing pairs and their nesting and roosting sites should be given maximum protection from disturbance . . . If possible, consider 'screening off' areas of farm buildings when

Young barn owls just can't help looking cute, especially when they use their flexible necks to get their heads into such odd positions. These two photogenic owlets were photographed at an old elm nest site in Hampshire. Thankfully, the value of dead elms as nest sites for owls (little and tawny as well as barn) is appreciated by many landowners, who will not fell them until they become too dangerous to be left standing.

owls are nesting (or roosting) and minimize your necessary work nearby as far as possible . . . Do not publicize the whereabouts of the birds unnecessarily.

In our experience, most farmers and landowners already take this careful and caring approach to their resident barn owls. As to the last

Barns at Titchwell earmarked for conversion to houses. A probable barn owl window can be seen in the apex of one of them. This sort of development is quite common nowadays, reflecting current government policy to encourage conversion of old farm buildings to domestic use. Town dwellers wishing to live in the country, even if it is only as commuters, will eagerly buy up an old barn and convert it into a 'desirable residence', as the estate agents would say. The disappearance of such barns is inevitable, it seems, and points up the need to provide alternative accommodation for barn owls.

point, taciturnity seems to be a congenital condition among farmers, and rightly so!

For its part, the BTO set up an Owl Study Group in 1988. To quote one of the OSG Newsletters:

> . . . the OSG has played a vital role in focusing enthusiasm for owls into standardized collection of good data. The project concentrated on tawny and barn owls, and both ringing and nest recording were boosted to impressive levels. Both species now generate sufficient nest data to allow between-year comparisons . . .

Owls as a group for study are particularly valuable because they are among what the BTO calls 'target species' as indicators of environmental change: if it is happening to owls, it is probably happening to other species too.

Another group which continues to do a great deal for the barn owl is the Hawk and Owl Trust. Their report, *The Barn Owl in the British Isles. Its Past, Present and Future*, which presents the findings of its Barn Owl survey (1982–85), led to the appointment of a full-time conservation officer and the establishment of a nationwide barn owl conservation network (BOCN), involving the services of Barn Owl specialists on a countrywide basis, to establish the Trust's Farmland, Riverside and Forestry Link schemes.

A key part of the Hawk and Owl Trust's barn owl conservation strategy is to create and maintain 'corridors' of rough grassland, six metres or more wide, alongside rivers, ditches, hedgerows and woodland. The purpose is to overcome the dangerous isolation of barn owl communities which are at the moment separated by unbroken stretches of monoculture prairies, and thereby to enable young birds to move in and maintain the population levels.

There are also many local initiatives currently concerned with improving the lot of the barn owl, especially among county wildlife trusts. The Cambridgeshire and Bedfordshire Wildlife Trust is typical. It has its own barn owl conservation programme with a vigorous nestbox scheme and an attractive promotional leaflet to encourage people to help. The county Trust's primary activity has been the erection of nestboxes: by the end of 1992 over 140 have been put up in suitable locations throughout the area. In fact the only limitation is finding suitable sites for the boxes, a point which we will take up later. An excellent aspect of the Trust's initiative is the cooperative nature of the venture. There has been enthusiastic support from local authorities: Cambridgeshire County Council has encouraged the erection of nestboxes on farms owned by the county, while Peterborough City Council has welcomed the Trust's assistance in its own 'Barn Owls, Bats and Buildings' project. There has also been excellent cooperation from such entities as the Forestry Commission, English Nature, the Hawk and Owl Trust and the Country Landowners' Association. The scheme has received some financial support, including a grant from the People's Trust for Endangered Species. Latterly, the sponsorship of the scheme has been taken over by Eastern Electricity. We have taken Cambridgeshire only as an example, for this kind of initiative is being repeated in

In Lincolnshire, a largely treeless landscape, pole-mounted boxes have been erected in pairs at 2 kilometre intervals east of Bourne, along the South Forty-foot Drain and the Glen River, from Pinchbeck northwards. They are mostly on land belonging to the National Rivers Authority, with a few on private farmland. The scheme, initiated and organized by the Hawk and Owl Trust, has met with some success, although occupation by other species is a problem. In the years 1989–92, there have been 70 jackdaw nests, 17 kestrel and 7 stock dove nests compared with 12 barn owl nests in the boxes. Various methods have been tried to exclude jackdaws in particular, including creating a baffle 'maze' within the box to prevent them taking twigs inside, lining the boxes with chippings and stopping up the roof sections with wire netting, as can be seen in the inset. Despite these setbacks, the scheme is adjudged a success, and is being extended into other areas where the only way to mount a nestbox for barn owls is to stick it on top of a pole.

other parts of Britain. It is a testimony to the remarkable appeal of
the barn owl. Perhaps, because of its spectacular appearance and its
place in folklore, it has become a symbol of what can be done to
reverse the destructive trends of the post-war era.

One of the most spectacular barn owl nestbox schemes is the one
which perches the boxes on top of old telegraph poles. The scheme
was started in 1984 by the Hawk and Owl Trust in conjunction with
the National Rivers Authority for the erection of pole-mounted
boxes in Lincolnshire and later in Yorkshire. One current project is
working with the Crown Commission to erect pole-mounted boxes
on Crown Commission land around Sandringham. Information on
the Lincolnshire pole-mounted boxes provided by Bob Sheppard,
who looks after the scheme in that county, gives an interesting
picture of the competition for these sites:

Year	89	90	91	92	
No. of boxes	16	16	42	42	Totals
Barn owl	4	3	2	3	12
Kestrel	3	2	8	4	17
Jackdaw	3	10	29	28	70
Stock dove	3	1	0	4	8
Tawny owl	0	0	1	2	3
Unoccupied	2	0	8	1	11
Broken	0	2	0	1	3
Not checked	1	0	0	0	1

Clearly, the barn owl benefits from these boxes, although the table
suggests that increasing the number of boxes does not increase the
number of breeding pairs of barn owls. It is also clear that this
nestbox scheme is proving of benefit to species we might approve of,
like kestrel and stock dove, and to species we might not, like
jackdaw. The occupation of two boxes in 1992 by tawny owls
reflects the shortage of natural tree sites. Multiple occupation occurs
too. We were told of one box which was occupied successively by
four different species in one season. It started with stock dove,
which were followed by a pair of jackdaws. The Trust cleared out
the jackdaw's nest, and barn owl took over, only to be followed
by kestrel!

Thus, an immense amount of energy goes into the provision of
nestbox sites for barn owls. What is the return on all this time and
effort? A study carried out by the Southwest Lancashire Ringing
Group provides some clues. Starting in the 1970s, they took as their
study area 44 square kilometres of low-lying, sparsely wooded,
arable farmland dissected by numerous drainage channels. A pre-
liminary survey indicated that there were, on average, 8 breeding

Checking a nestbox in a barn can be a hazardous business, not only because of the height at which the box needs to be placed, but also because of the malodorous state of the nest, which can take your breath away. This shot shows Jake inspecting the Church Barn nest, checking to see that the five bonny chicks inside are doing well. They were, and all five fledged despite relatively poor vole numbers and a prolonged wet spell that summer. The dark interior of the barn presented lighting problems for the photographer, and physical problems for Jake, who was required to remain totally still for eight seconds in a situation where his natural instinct was to shake with fear!

pairs in the study area, giving a breeding density of 1.8 pairs per 10 square kilometres. The group then erected 37 nestboxes in the study area, mostly modified tea-chests. The results of their survey show that, in a good year, up to 19 per cent of the boxes are used for breeding and 47 per cent for roosting. The number of breeding pairs recorded varied over a 13-year period between 1 and 9 pairs, giving a breeding density of between 0.23 and 2.05 pairs per 10 square kilometres. From these figures, it is clear that the provision of nestboxes did not increase the breeding density. So what did the nestbox scheme achieve? Jerry Seymour of the group, in a report on the project published in *BTO News*, makes this comment:

What nestboxes may do . . . is to cause owls to switch to safer breeding sites, thus enabling them to successfully raise more young. Before the erection of nestboxes, many birds attempted to breed upon straw bales, often failing as bales were moved by farmers.

Moreover, the increased fledging rate means that the number of potential breeding barn owls increases too. Seymour's report concludes:

Our results suggest that 2.05 pairs per 10 square kilometres is a maximum breeding density and that where this is achieved, young birds are chased out of the study area and establish territories in adjoining areas.

One of the most controversial aspects in this surge of activity to help the barn owl has been the releasing into the wild of captive-bred birds. Estimates of the number of birds bred in captivity are truly staggering. An article in *Cage and Aviary Birds* in December 1990 written by David Ramsden (conservation officer, Barn Owl Trust) revealed that the British Bird Council supplied 6,130 closed rings for captive-bred barn owls in 1990, and estimated that the total number of barn owls in captivity was between 20,000 and 30,000. In contrast, current population estimates for birds in the wild stands at about 9,000. How many of these captive-bred birds are released into the wild, and under what conditions? In the 24 February 1992 issue of *The Times*, under the poignant headline 'Misguided saviours send owls to their death', the paper's environment correspondent, Michael McCarthy, wrote:

About 600 well-intentioned but misguided amateur breeders have been releasing up to 3,000 captive-bred barn owls into the wild each year . . . According to the RSPB, they have almost invariably wasted their time and the birds' lives, since 90 per cent do not survive their first year.

This sort of death rate is unacceptably high, although we should remember that ringing studies show that the percentage of wild barn owls dying in their first year is rarely less than 60 per cent, and is often much higher.

There are several methods for releasing a captive-bred young barn owl into the wild. The most reprehensible, and one which is only practised by ignorant individuals, is to toss the bird out of the car window into the nearest likely-looking bit of countryside, with or without a prayer for its future. The two methods which take the best account of the need for the young birds to adapt to their environment and learn to fend for themselves are called 'long-term release' and 'young clutch release'. In the first, a pair of captive-bred owls are confined in a suitably adapted building for a period of months and allowed to breed. When the young are about four weeks old, the adults are removed and supplementary feeding is continued for a period of months. In the second, a brood of five-week-old chicks is placed in a nestbox inside the building and is then fed for several months. But, even when the greatest care is taken to acclimatize the young birds, there is one overriding factor to consider: the suitability

The parent bird has just come out of the nestbox having fed the young, which are visible inside the box. These are some of the famous Fairchild's brood of eight. The platform on which the adult is standing is an essential part of the design of the nestbox, as it will be used by the owlets as a safe area to exercise before venturing into the wider world beyond. In fact, two of them flipflopped their way down to the floor of the barn at an early stage. Full of concern, we put them carefully back into the nest, only to find them on the ground again when we returned next day. As they seemed safe and happy, we did not bother to return them again, and they eventually fledged along with the rest.

of the proposed release area. Is there already a pair of barn owls in that locality? If so, it would be bad practice to disturb them. If not, is the absence of birds an indication that there is a lack of suitable feeding habitat? What other hazards are there in the vicinity?

An example of a well-thought-out release scheme is the one practised by the New Forest Owl Sanctuary, whose leaflet sets out their method:

Great care is taken over releasing owls into the wild. There must be suitable nesting sites and hunting terrain, and someone who will accept responsibility for the owl until it attains full independence. The owls leave the sanctuary at the age of five to six weeks, about three weeks before they can fly, so they have to be fed and protected until they can fully fend for themselves.

Unfortunately, responsible schemes of that kind are the exception. To combat irresponsible releasing of young barn owls into the wild, the government, on the same day that *The Times* article appeared, announced that the barn owl had been added to Schedule 9 of the

Wildlife and Countryside Act, bringing it into line with other raptors. It means that, henceforth, people wishing to release barn owls into the wild can only do so under licence. From our conversations with affected parties, it seems that the licensing scheme is bureaucratically cumbersome – and somewhat irritating to reputable organizations which have been operating responsible breed-and-release schemes. Nonetheless, the addition of barn owl to Schedule 9 was long overdue. It is to be hoped that, from now on, every introduction of captive-bred birds into the wild will take full account of the welfare of the birds and of the environmental factors which will enable such releases to make a genuine contribution to the maintenance and expansion of breeding barn owls in Britain.

A note on nestbox construction

There is no shortage of information on constructing and locating nestboxes for barn owls. A random survey turned up the following:

The BTO in conjunction with the Hawk and Owl Trust has produced a series of leaflets called *Artificial Nest Sites for Birds of Prey* covering the owls and birds of prey like kestrels. Leaflet Number 2 is *Barn Owl*. In addition to the standard barn-site box with the tray in front for the young to exercise, this leaflet gives a specification for pole-mounted boxes.

The Hawk and Owl Trust has a number of leaflets covering various aspects of barn owl conservation. For the construction of nestboxes, there is *Nest Boxes for Barn Owls*. In addition, there is an excellent leaflet called *Building for Barn Owls*, which gives tips on creating owl windows and how to construct an owl loft. For the ambitious or those who live in treeless landscapes, the Trust leaflet *Specification for Pole Boxes* is required reading.

The RSPB has a leaflet called *Nestboxes for Less Common Birds* which covers barn owl and kestrel, but also such mouth-watering species as goldeneye, pied flycatcher, redstart and nuthatch. Their leaflet *Barn Owl Nestbox Scheme* is useful in that it gives information, with illustrations, on how to make nestboxes not only from 6 millimetre marine ply, which is waterproof but expensive, but also, more cheaply, from tea-chests and wooden barrels, which can only be used in dry locations, of course.

For those people who cannot cut a slice of bread let alone saw marine ply into accurate sections, the alternative is to cough up about £30

Figure 4: Constructing a barn owl nestbox

and buy a ready-to-make-up box from a specialist manufacturer. For our own boxes, we try to keep expense to a minimum: tea-chests at 50 pence each from our local tip – sorry, recycling centre and landfill site – and wood for the lids and trays from the bits left behind by a local undertaker!

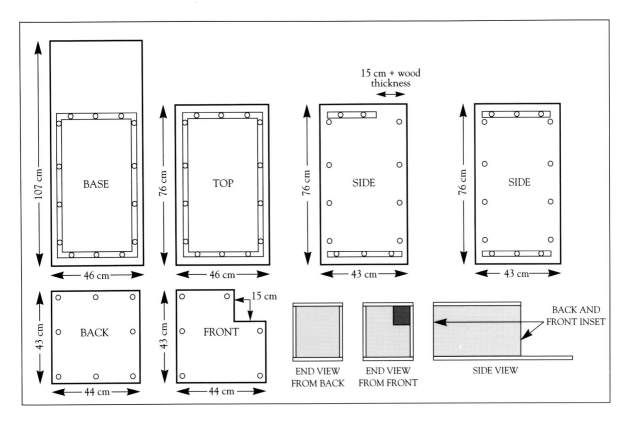

11 Barn Owls in Folklore and Legend

**Harbinger of Death and illness,
Fatal Bellman, Bird of Doom . . .**

Owls, silent and mysterious creatures of the night, have always been closely associated with magic and witchcraft. Witness the witches' brew in *Macbeth*, which would not have been complete without its bit of owl:

> Lizard's leg and howlet's wing,
> For a charm of powerful trouble,
> Like a hell-broth boil and bubble.

With its combination of ghostly pallor and eldritch shriek, and its association with churchyards, the barn owl is perhaps the quint-essential owl of popular imagination. The many names by which it is known reflect its attributes, real or supposed. To capture its coloration, it is called, variously, white, silver or yellow owl. In Gaelic, it is *cailleach-oidhche gheal*, 'White Hag of the Night'. In Spain, its milky colour gives it the name *lechuza* (Spanish *leche* = milk).

To reflect its famous or infamous shriek, it is called, variously, screech, scritch or screaming owl. Francesca Greenoak recorded the name hissing owl in Yorkshire, reflecting another of its characteristic vocalizations. The general Welsh name for an owl, *gwdihŵ*, probably echoes tawny owl; barn owl is *tylluan sgubor*, which is literally 'barn owl'. We like the Manx name *screeaghag oie*.

In the Lesser Antilles, the barn owl has the charming name *chat-huant*, French for 'hooting cat' (*Chat-huant* is also an alternative name in France for *hulotte*, i.e. tawny owl). Is it fanciful to hear echoes of sounds made by the bird in the Russian name *sipukha*, the guttural 'kh' so vividly rendering the hissing or snoring sound made by indignant or hungry nestlings? Or the name in Xhosa, *Isixhova*? Xhosa is an African click language, containing the 'xh' sound made by barn owls when they click their tongues, usually in aggressive display. The word 'owl' itself is derived from a proto-Indoeuropean verb meaning 'to howl' (compare French *hibou*, German *Eule*, Dutch *Uil*), and several dialect names derived from 'owl' are wonderfully onomatopoeic: woolert, hoolet, hullart and ullat. Variants on 'owl'

Mike didn't actually aim to repeat the famous Eric Hosking shot of a barn owl in heraldic pose, but was delighted when he developed a film taken at Fairchild's and discovered that he had achieved not one, but two, successive shots of a 'heraldic' bird. In the first shot, the bird was carrying a wood mouse, and in the second, seen here, a short-tailed vole. The Hosking picture has sold in 106 countries. Mike is very hopeful.

are preserved in a number of placenames, including Ullswater in Cumbria and Olcoates in Nottinghamshire.

Despite its association with gloom and doom, it is, in common with other familiar birds like robin redbreast, magpie and jackdaw, sometimes given a friendly personal name such as the north country Jenny owl, the Gill hooter of Cheshire, the East Anglian Madge howlet, and the charming Norfolk name, Billy wise. This may not indicate affection, though, so much as the sort of nervous appeasing jocularity that caused people to refer to the Devil as 'Old Nick'. There was a time, too, when barn owls and tawny owls had a more angelic reputation, when they were known respectively as Cherubim and Seraphim, those plump little angels whose cheeky bottoms and puffy cheeks adorn the frames of so many religious pictures. But maybe any resemblance to owls in this case is purely coincidental.

Reflecting its morbid associations, the barn owl is known in some parts of the world, in the West Indies, for example, as the death bird. In Shakespeare, one of the omens of Julius Caesar's impending doom is a barn owl, made all the more sinister by appearing in broad daylight:

> . . . yesterday, the bird of night did sit
> Even at noonday, upon the market place,
> Hooting and shrieking.

The association of barn owls with church towers and graveyards has given rise to all sorts of legends about the bird as a portent of death and ill omen. Among the many vernacular names which associate the barn owl with such matters, the Welsh *Aderyn corff*, literally corpse bird, is perhaps the most lugubrious.

Pliny, quoted in Sparks and Soper's book, identifies the barn owl as the bird of ill omen and does not mince his words:

> The scritch-owle betokeneth always some heavy news, and is most execrable and accursed in the presaging of public affairs . . . he is the very monster of the night, neither crying nor singing out clear, but uttering a certain groan of doleful moaning. And, therefore, if he be seen either within cities or otherwise abroad in any place, it is not for good, but prognosticates some fearful misfortune.

In this vein, a sample of adjectives taken from various poets sums up the poor old owl's perceived character. At best, he is 'grave' and 'solemn': this is the 'wise old owl' end of the spectrum. Soon, though, his character becomes unattractive: he is 'dismal' and 'dull', 'moody' and 'moping', 'sullen' and 'sad'. Finally, he degenerates into unholiness: he is 'grim', he is 'ghostly', he is 'spectral', he is 'curst'. From Chaucer to Scott, from Shakespeare to Keats, our bird is maligned:

> The owle at night about the balkes word
> That prophete is of wo and mischaunce (Chaucer)

> Birds of omen, dark and foul (Scott)

> . . . shrieking harbinger,
> Foul precursor of the fiend (Shakespeare)

> Gloom bird's hated screech (Keats)

Even when the barn owl is not announcing death or illness, all sorts of other nefarious practices are attributed to it. Joaquim Maluquer i Sostres, in *Els Ocells de les Terres Catalanes*, records a persistent belief amongst the normally level-headed Catalans:

> *L'òliba viu prop dels llocs habitats, i molt sovint nia a les torres i als campanars, cosa que va donar origen a l'absurda creença que aquest ocell xuclava l'oli de les llànties de les esglésies.*

The barn owl lives near human habitations, and very often nests in towers and belfries, which gave rise to the absurd belief that this bird used to suck the oil from lamps in churches.

The barn owl could prove useful to MI5 in dealing with captured spies, or perhaps to those eternally optimistic TV folk who interview politicians. E. A. Armstrong, in his book *The Folklore of Birds*, tells us that, 'If you lay the heart and right foot of a barn owl on one who is asleep, he will answer whatever you ask him and tell what he has done.' It is apparently of even greater value to a suspicious husband: he should put the owl's bits on his spouse's left breast while she is sleeping and have the tape recorder ready for when she wakes up and starts blurting out the truth about the housekeeping, the milkman, or . . . but this is not a nice subject, so we will leave it at that.

Just as there is white magic as well as black magic, the barn owl, if properly propitiated, can be an influence for good. In Italy, for example, the best way to counteract *il malocchio*, the evil eye, was, and in country villages still is, to nail an owl above the barn door. Interestingly, given that it is often blamed for bringing illness, the barn owl is also used sometimes as a cure. Given that a barn owl's hoot is as good as a whoop, what better way to get rid of whooping cough than a nice dish of owl broth? Similarly, just as the young Masai must kill a lion and then drink its blood to imbibe the animal's strength and courage, there was a time when you could not improve on a meal of powdered barn owls' eggs if you wanted to improve your eyesight. According to one classical writer, the effect of eating an owl's egg is to put you off wine for life. The authors of this book wish to place on record that they have never eaten an owl's egg, and, having found out about the last piece of folk medicine, are never likely to. We may laugh nowadays at these absurd superstitions, but it is no laughing matter when rhinos continue to be killed for the supposed aphrodisiac properties of their horns; or when thousands of Chinese black bears are kept in cages so cramped that the poor creatures eventually and literally go mad, and all because the Chinese believe that the bear's bile has magical curative properties.

Earlier in the book, we have addressed questions like: Why is the barn owl pale? Why is the barn owl nocturnal? Why does it shriek so? Folklore provides much more colourful answers than ours. The barn owl is, of course, really a baker's daughter, who brought woe upon herself by eating bread which her mother had baked for Jesus. The bread swelled up inside her and she began to choke, uttering shrieks like an owl, which was appropriate, because by then she had turned into one. The barn owl was not always a night bird, but it forfeited the privilege of living in the daylight because of its unforgivable behaviour. There are two versions to choose from, depending on

The east window of Stickney church in Lincolnshire. The owls in the upper panels are reputed to be barn owls but, if they are, they are highly stylized! They are in classic heraldic pose, which is described in Fox-Davies's *Complete Guide to Heraldry* as 'always depicted with the face affronté, though the body is not usually so placed'. Underneath the east window there is a plaque describing its symbolism:

In memory of the Reverend George Henry Hales, Assistant Curate of Stickney 1879 to 1883. Rector 1883 to 1922. Under the centre figure of our Lord are Angels upholding the scroll, on which is inscribed the text: "Bless the Lord ye that excel in strength, hearkening unto the voice of His word". In the upper lights are shown the arms of Eton and Trinity College Cambridge, where he was educated. Beneath these are depicted the rooks, such as built in the trees about the Rectory, and the owls which inhabited the Church Tower. When the latter was rebuilt in 1900, special entrances were planned, that they might still nest there.

The only other sacred barn owl we know of is in the chantry of Bishop Oldham at Exeter, where the owl, representing the first syllable of Oldham (ol = owl), has a label in its beak charged with the letters dom, representing the second syllable. The borough of Oldham in Lancashire bears arms containing three owls.

whether you like your barn owls banished for meanness or skulking in the shadows out of shame. Was the barn owl banished to night by the king for refusing to obey his command that it, along with all the other species of bird, should give a feather to a shivering wren which had lost its own? Or was it ashamed that it had fallen asleep when told, by a different king presumably, to guard a wren which had been imprisoned for the improbable offence of flying higher than an eagle (it had done this by perching on the eagle's tail)?

As to its ghostly or spectral appearance, it belongs with the will-o'-

the-wisps and the jack-o'-lanterns that spook the marshes and scare good folk out of their wits. In fact, barn owls really can 'glow' at times. A particularly luminous barn owl was seen by Norfolk observers and reported in the transactions of their local naturalists' society:

> ... on February 3, 1907, on reaching the top of Twyford Hill, we noticed a light apparently moving in the direction of Wood Norton ... After moving horizontally backwards and forwards several hundred yards, it rose in the air to the height of forty feet or more ... The light was slightly reddish in the centre, and resembled a carriage lamp, for which we at first mistook it. We watched it for twenty minutes and were quite at a loss to ascertain its cause. The light emerged across the field, at times approaching within fifty yards of where I was standing. It then alighted on the ground for a few seconds. A slight mist hung over the ground. On another occasion, the evening being dark, the bird issued from a covert. Its luminosity seemed to have increased and it literally lighted up the branches of the trees as it flew past them ...

From the writer's concluding comments (below), we may assume that his fellow members did not believe him, and can take comfort from the fact that nothing much has changed in the cut-throat world of county natural history societies since his day:

> I have recorded these observations merely in the hope that some naturalist may be found whose scientific attainments will enable him to elucidate the cause of a highly interesting natural phenomenon, and thereby refute the contemptible assertions of those who pour ridicule on everything they have not seen themselves, to the great detriment of scientific research.

The explanation for this curiosity favoured by Bunn et al is that barn owls sometimes roost in hollow trees where luminous bacteria and honey fungus, also occasionally luminous, are present. Fine particles adhere to the feathering, and hey presto! a glowing barn owl emerges to reinforce its image of mystery and other-worldliness.

Despite its ancient reputation as the bad news bird, the barn owl has been used occasionally as a heraldic device, notably in the town arms of Dewsbury, Leeds and Oldham. In its role as a wise bird, it is sometimes used as a school badge, as at Manchester Grammar School. Nowadays, its reputation restored, the barn owl has become one of our most popular birds. Its image is widely used as a symbol of excellence and sagacity to sell everything from computers to insurance and reproduced in every medium from papier mâché to Royal Doulton china.

12 An Interview with the Photographer

Active watch our friend is keeping,
Doing work no other can . . .

JAKE: Perhaps we can start by talking about your use of flash in doing the photography for this book. I guess that flash is not there simply to put a light on the bird, but to create special effects as well. Can you give me some examples of how you used flash to create effects?

MIKE: Well, the shot of the bird landing at the hay bales [p. 95], for instance, has one flash gun filling in on the camera side of the bird, and that is slightly further away than the two flash guns giving the backlighting. I think this gives a more ethereal, night-time feel to the photograph, plus, of course, better modelling of the subject. Compare it with the little owl [p. 114] which is obviously a daylight image backlit by the setting sun. The barn owl photograph is simulating the same effect, but the black background and the rest of the make-up of the picture tells you that it is a night-time shot.

JAKE: Is the barn owl shot an example of where the bird has taken its own photograph, as it were, by breaking an infra-red beam?

MIKE: Yes. In fact, many of the in-flight shots are.

JAKE: How do you determine where to put the infra-red beam? Do you make a guess, and move it if your guess is not quite right?

MIKE: You can do that, but generally you start by sitting and watching. One snag is that with standard cameras there is about a 1/10th of a second delay between the breaking of the beam and the firing of the flash, which means that, in that time, the bird will have travelled a good 30 to 60 centimetres. What you have to do is to set the beam up in such a way that it allows for the delay so that the bird will fly through the beam and then into frame, by which time it will be taking its own photograph.

JAKE: I guess it can be frustrating sometimes. I remember at the Church Barn, when you were trying to photograph the bird coming out over the half-door, it was possible for the bird actually to come out without breaking the beam, wasn't it?

Little owl on fencepost, backlit by setting sun. This kind of shot generally needs a lot of careful preparation to get the subject in exactly the right place at exactly the right time. The backlit cobwebs add further interest to the composition. How this difficult shot was achieved is described in this chapter.

MIKE: That's right. It was a large barn and the bird could easily miss the beam. It's not only a matter of predicting the point of focus, but also of anticipating the route the bird will take. With day flying birds, it is much easier to see what is happening and then make any necessary adjustments.

JAKE: Returning to the back-lit little owl for the moment, this is a shot which depends entirely on natural light. How did you manage to get that?

MIKE: Well, that was a case of manipulation of the subject combined with natural light. I wanted to get a shot of an owl on a post backlit by the setting sun. Little owl proved to be the easiest one to work with, but the lighting conditions were very difficult. The bird was backlit and I was probably getting some sun straight on to the lens as well, so I was getting an exposure reading that was too high for the camera-side part of the owl and the fence post.

JAKE: In other words, it would have come out much too dark?

MIKE: Yes, but the sky would have been nicely exposed! I had to compensate by opening up one and a third stops to end up with a nicely rim-lit owl, backlit at sunset, with the spiders' webs nicely glistening as well.

JAKE: You mentioned manipulation of the subject. What is that about?

MIKE: Manipulation of the subject means persuading the subject to be where you want it and to do what you want it to do for the purposes of photography. In the case of the little owl, it was manipulation in the nicest possible way. It was a totally wild little owl. I put bait on the fence post day after day after day until the weather was right. In fact I went down to the farm every day for about four weeks putting food out on the post, trying photographs on one or two suitable evenings, but mostly just getting down there, observing, and waiting for the weather to improve.

JAKE: There's another photograph which depended on natural light, but where you had an immense problem. I mean the one showing the interior of the Church Barn with me up a ladder inspecting the nestbox [p. 101].

MIKE: Yes, it was really too dark inside the barn for photography. Anyway, I positioned myself on the other side of the barn, although not as high as you. What I did was to climb up the ladder to get to the lower part of a diagonal, and then jammed my tripod over that to hold it nice and steady. The photograph is in fact an 8-second exposure. That's how dark it was in the barn! One thing I like about it is that there is the open door with light spilling into the barn from there. I think that gives a lovely quality to the light in that particular barn. It's all underlit.

JAKE: Is it all right if I, as the chap up the ladder, describe the total agony of having to remain frozen in that position for eight seconds – are you sure it was only eight? – with my nose stuck in a nestbox that seemed to be giving off ammonia fumes!

MIKE: Go ahead! The three things that amaze me about the photograph are, first, that it has come out at all, and it's come out correctly exposed. Second, that there wasn't any camera shake on it. There you've got an eight-second exposure with me up a ladder that moves about and the tripod leaning against me and the ladder, I'm surprised that didn't give us any movement – mind you, I did throw quite a few away. Finally, that you didn't move at all. I don't know whether it was that you were so scared that you didn't dare to move . . .

JAKE: I was paralysed! Can I ask a general question about lighting in relation to the barn owl? This is a bird of darkness, and the bird itself is pale, so a lot of photography of barn owls that I've seen is basically black and white. How have you managed to get so much colour and so much detail?

MIKE: Some of it is the use of surroundings, if you like. But the barn owl is quite colourful. While it's basically white in the front, when you look at its back, it's not. To get some colour and texture, it's a matter of sidelighting rather than head-on lighting.

JAKE: There is one shot which must have been particularly difficult to do and that is one at the Church Barn, and that is where you've got the bird coming out of what is basically a black stable door.

MIKE: It is a difficult situation, where I was trying to retain detailing in the barn owl, and also to get detailing in the barn. It's a no-win situation. I'd end up with either a totally burnt-out barn owl and lots of detail in the black, or no detailing in the black but lots of detailing in the bird. Now, the way that I tried to overcome it is to have some detailing on the roof, and some detailing of the vegetation by the barn door, a little bit of the wall and the white droppings down the door. On the way out, the bird broke the infra-red beam and was at the focal point, i.e. at the stable door, when the photograph was taken. I've used four flashguns: one down low to light the door and the vegetation, one at medium height to light the barn owl, and another one quite a bit higher up to light part of the roof as well. The fourth flash was to the other side to give a bit of modelling, a bit of fill-in light.

JAKE: Did you have any lighting inside the barn itself?

MIKE: No. I could have put another set of flashguns inside to light the inside wall of the barn, but I don't think that would have looked right. I think the barn owl coming out of the darkness is much more dramatic.

JAKE: You must have taken a lot of shots in order to get just the one you wanted. What's the wastage rate in this kind of photography?

MIKE: With the photograph of the bird coming over the stable door, I got three shots which I thought were acceptable, one of which is better than the other two, and that is the one which appears in the book. I think I took only thirty shots in all to get those three.

JAKE: Only? It sounds like a lot to me.

MIKE: Not really. I could devote only a limited amount of time and effort to that particular shot. So, a one-in-ten strike rate is pretty good.

JAKE: What's your estimate of the general strike rate, as you call it?

MIKE: For the in-flight photography, if you get one-in-ten, you're doing well. If one-in-twenty, you're still doing quite well.

JAKE: What this tells me is that, after you have used all your skill and experience and all your ingenuity in setting up, there is still that element of chance to give you the shot where everything comes together, the resolution, the positioning of the bird, and so on.

MIKE: That's right. It's not really luck, because I think you work to make your own luck. But whether the birds wings are exactly as you want them – horizontal or five degrees up or down, for instance – is just a matter of the way the bird works. If it takes off into a wind, its reactions will be different from taking off with the wind or on a very calm day.

JAKE: I'd like to ask you about shots you've got which you are really pleased with, but which you didn't actually think you were going to get. Has that happened to you while working on this book?

MIKE: Yes, and it happened not once, but twice in succession on a roll of film. There's a very famous Eric Hosking shot of a barn owl in heraldic pose, front view in flight, wings raised above its body. Now, I didn't actually aim to repeat that, so you can imagine my surprise when two successive images on one roll of film showed exactly that. This was at the Fairchild's nest. And there they were: two shots in a row of the bird in heraldic pose, virtually identical to the Hosking picture. At first, I was mystified: how come the

Sometimes in photography as in life, the best laid plans 'gang aft agley'. The shot of a chick swallowing whole prey, in this case a short-tailed vole, did not seem to present a particular challenge. In fact, every time this event occurred, captured in this photograph, the female chose to upstage her offspring by standing between it and the camera.

camera took two shots on one take-off? Did it do a double exposure, or what? On closer examination, I was able to determine that in one shot the bird had a wood mouse in its beak, and in the other a short-tailed vole [p. 106]. So it was two separate and successive visits to the nest which ended up virtually identical except for the prey item!

JAKE: You said earlier that you make your own luck, and part of that must be that you sometimes persuade your subject to do what you want it to do. You gave an example earlier of four weeks spent baiting up a fence post just to persuade a little owl to perch on it. Can you give us another example of this kind of 'manipulating'?

MIKE: Well, I suppose the cattle trough shot is a good example [p. 84]. Barn owls occasionally die by drowning in cattle troughs. When photographers want to portray that, they will find a dead barn owl in a cattle trough or get a road casualty and put it in a trough, then just point the camera down and take a photograph of it in there. That's fine, but I wanted something a bit more imaginative. So I decided to try getting down to the barn owl's level when it's in the water. The only way I could do that was to find an old trough, cut off one end and replace the end with a glass panel, and photograph through the glass panel looking upwards within the trough.

JAKE: You even got a cow looking into the trough! Was that manipulation, too?

MIKE: Yes, the lady who owned the field persuaded the cows to come over and drink from the trough while I clicked away. There was a snag, though, in that the cattle drank so much that the water level fell very rapidly! It had only to fall by a centimetre for the shot to alter dramatically, so we had to keep topping the water up to maintain the right level.

JAKE: But in the end you got the dramatic shot you were striving for. Everything you have said underlines the immense amount of time and effort that has gone into the photography for this book. What constraints were you working under?

MIKE: Before anything else, I would mention that barn owl is on Schedule One of the Wildlife and Countryside Act, which means that you need a special permit from English Nature to approach a nest. Photography permits are issued on a quota basis. I was lucky to get permits for two successive seasons, but I was fully aware that I might not get a third, so I felt under some pressure to get the shots I wanted. Added to this is the fact that you need to be able to take a variety of shots, and so you need a variety of setups. Even at the Fairchild's site, we had two hides set up, one on the outside of the barn to photograph the comings and goings of the birds, and

At this barn owl nest site, we had hides both inside and outside the nesting barn, which is to the right of the hide in this shot. The outside hide enabled us to get flight shots of the birds arriving at the barn. It is essential with hide photography to erect the hide a little at a time, moving it in stages closer to the site to ensure that the birds get used to it. In this case, the birds were so used to the coming and going of heavy pieces of farm equipment near their site that they took no notice at all of the hides. Indeed, as the droppings show, they used it as a perch at times, which was convenient for them but no good at all for our photography!

one on the inside of the barn to photograph activity at the nesting box. As to the setting up of hides, well, you can't just set them up and go and sit in them. You have to start building the hide either at a distance or little by little every day and check that the birds accept that. Just setting up the hide outside the Fairchild's barn was three or four evenings' work. Not only that, but we also put up false flashguns so that when photography does start, the change to real flashguns causes minimal disturbance to the birds. And, of course, once you are ready to use the hide, someone has to see you into it and out again at the end of the session, so that the birds, if they are watching, will see a human being walk away at the beginning of the session, and will be naturally disturbed, so to speak, when that person returns to the hide to get the photographer out. A photographer appearing out of a hide could cause the birds to become nervous, suspicious of the hide, or, even worse, to desert.

JAKE: What about the birds' reactions to the flash of the lights and the clicking of the camera shutter during photography?

MIKE: Of course these things have an effect. When I am first sitting in the hide, I tend to watch the birds and assess their reactions to the replacing of the false camera lens and false flashguns with real ones. Providing they do not appear to be disturbed, as they arrive and depart I make a clicking noise with my tongue just to see if they are bothered by sounds. Since barn owls are immensely wary, a mechanical sound like the noise of a camera is something that

A barn owl just inside the entrance to a potential nesting site. It is in typical roosting pose, standing on one leg, eyes almost closed. Doing nothing seems to be the barn owl's preferred activity. This can be very frustrating for the observer who, however dedicated, begins to experience a sense of futility and unreality as the hours pass by with the observed bird offering little more frenzied than the occasional scratch, stretch or shuffle.

they tend to accept more than, say, a slight movement of my foot inside the hide. So if I shuffled my position, that was more of a disturbance to them than the click of the camera. When you're doing the photography, you have to watch the birds and gauge their reactions. If they overreact, don't take any more photographs that session, switch everything off, just sit and watch and enjoy the comings and goings.

JAKE: You find that your birds get used to being photographed?

MIKE: Yes, if you introduce things gradually and allow the birds to accept things in a very relaxed way, then you don't wind them up. You get relaxed birds and good photography.

JAKE: What was it like working from a hide at night?

MIKE: I enjoyed it. Sitting in a hide in a barn in the dark was a bit claustrophobic, and I never knew when the birds were going to arrive, but I enjoy the challenge of trying to get the ultimate photograph. One of the big snags with barn owl photography is that you cannot move or make any noise in the hide. I remember one evening, having sat in the hide for three or four hours, I hadn't moved my feet or my legs at all, and what I hadn't realized was that one of my legs had gone totally dead. As I tried to clamber out of the hide, I couldn't tell whether my foot was on the ground or still in mid-air. It was the weirdest sensation.

JAKE: Finally, can you say something about the equipment you use?

MIKE: My cameras are Canon T90s, and I use a variety of Canon lenses. Much of the owl photography was done with a 70–210 zoom lens, a few were done with a wide-angle lens, and one or two with a 400 millimetre lens. A lot of the photography was done from a hide and the camera was tripod-mounted for steadiness. The tripods I use are much heavier than those used by most birdwatchers. This helps to reduce camera shake especially when using a long lens. The film used has been mostly Fuji Velvia, which is a 50 ISO film, and there are a few taken on Kodachrome 64. I use these slow films because their fine grain is best for reproduction purposes. Then, because most of the photography was done at night, I obviously had to use flash. I have a quantity of Sunpack Auto 36DX flash guns. These have variable power, which means that on 1/4 power, I can freeze the movement of a flying barn owl. In some cases, the flash has been used to front light the birds, but usually I either side lit or back lit them.

JAKE: Thank you, Mike, for sharing some of the secrets of your barn owl photography with us.

Parent bird returning to nest with wood mouse. The nearby field had just been harvested, with the result that the owls had an easy time for several days. They rarely needed to fly further than a few yards, and were returning with prey at two to three minute intervals for the first part of the night.

123

The Barn Owl, a Plea for its Protection

This poem was written around the beginning of the century by Mike Read's great great uncle, George Bentley Corbin, whose obituary appeared in *The Times* in 1914. The poem is from a locally published collection entitled *Stray Leaves from the Avon Valley, Hampshire*.

When the twilight mingling sweetly
With the night the stars reveal,
Dor and bat and night-hawk featly
From their hiding places steal;
All who would the daylight shun
Now their revels have begun.

Round the haystacks, o'er the meadows,
Stubble fields, and hedgerow sides,
Weird and white – among the shadows
Silently some creature glides,
Buoyant, calm, and lack of noise;
What the purpose of its poise?

Harbinger of Death and illness,
Fatal Bellman, Bird of Doom,
Coming near sick chamber's stillness,
Holding converse with the tomb;
Evil omens wreath its name,
Nothing good surrounds its fame.

Superstition blindly ready
With bold ignorance to bind,
Fear's dread fetters, firm and steady,
Grossly lying, – here we find;
Guardian more than culprit he,
Zealous in his industry.

Spare! nor heed the common tattle,
Learn the truth and strive to know
Those who give this night-bird battle
Kill a friend and call him foe.
Game-preserver, farmer, all
Might him Benefactor call.

Far more potent – working duly –
Than best trap, or cruel gin,
Nature's balance, weighing truly
Mice and their marauding kin;
Squeak or rustle in the straw
Met by an unerring claw!

Eye and ear both wonder winning,
Hearing as acute as sight,
Plumage soft as silkworm's spinning,
Fringèd wings and noiseless flight.
Beak set in a disk-like face,
Character of all the race.

Clad in white, and buff – grey-blended, –
Wise of visage; is it true
Greek Minerva condescended
Oft' to have this bird in view?
Now, forgetful of his use,
Persecute we the recluse.

In the ivied ruin hoary,
Hollow trunk, or steeple grey,
There he sits in solemn glory
Dozing through the livelong day,
But as darkness draweth near
This grand mouser has no peer.

Thus, while the world is sleeping,
(How short-sighted oft' is man) –
Active watch our friend is keeping,
Doing work no other can,
Costing nought: his recompense
Murder! is it common sense?

Bibliography

General

BUNN D.S., WARBURTON A.B. and WILSON R.D.S. *The Barn Owl* (T. & A.D. Poyser, 1982)
CORBIN George Bentley *Stray Leaves from the Avon Valley, Hampshire* (Private Publication)
CRAMP S. ed. *The Birds of the Western Palearctic Vol IV* (OUP, 1985)
EVERETT Michael *A Natural History of Owls* (Hamlyn, 1977)
HARRIS A., TUCKER L., VINICOMBE K. *The Macmillan Field Guide to Bird Identification* (Macmillan, 1989)
HUDSON W.H. *Adventures among Birds* (J.M. Dent and Sons Ltd, 1923)
LEACH Michael *The Complete Owl* (Chatto and Windus, London, 1992)
MARTIN Graham *Birds by Night* (T. & A.D. Poyser, 1990)
MEAD Chris *Owls* (Whittet Books, 1987)
MIKKOLA Heimo *Owls of Europe* (T. & A.D. Poyser, 1983)
SPARKS J. and SOPER Tony *Owls – Their Natural and Unnatural History* (David and Charles, 1970)
TOOPS Connie *The Enchanting Owl* (Swan Hill Press, 1990)

Conservation

BRAZIL M.A. and SHAWYER C.R. *The Barn Owl The Farmer's Friend Needs a Helping Hand* (The Hawk Trust, 1989)
BRITISH TRUST FOR ORNITHOLOGY *Artificial Nest Sites for Birds of Prey: 2, Barn Owl* (Undated Leaflet)
CAYFORD J. 'Barn Owl Ecology on East Anglian Farmland' (Report in *RSPB Conservation Review* 6, 1992)
HAWK AND OWL TRUST 'The Future of the Barn Owl in Britain' *Report of the First National Barn Owl Conservation Network Symposium* 1989
HAWK AND OWL TRUST *Building for Barn Owls* (Undated Leaflet)
HAWK AND OWL TRUST *Specification for Pole Boxes* (Undated Leaflet)
ROYAL SOCIETY FOR THE PROTECTION OF BIRDS *Barn Owl Nestbox Scheme* (Undated Leaflet)
ROYAL SOCIETY FOR THE PROTECTION OF BIRDS *Nestboxes for Less Common Birds* (Undated Leaflet)
SHAW Geoff & DOWELL A. 'Barn Owl Conservation in Forests' *Forestry Commission Bulletin 90* (HMSO, 1990)
SHAWYER C.R. *The Barn Owl in the British Isle, Its Past, Present and Future* (The Hawk Trust, 1987)

Diet

YALDEN D.W. *The Identification of Remains in Owl Pellets* (Occasional Publication of the Mammal Society, undated).
YALDEN D.W. and MORRIS P.A. *The Analysis of Owl Pellets* (Occasional Publication of the Mammal Society: No 13, 1990)

Description

GINN H.B. & MELVILLE D.S. *Moult in Birds* (BTO Guide No. 19, 1983)
WITHERBY H.F. et al *Handbook of British Birds, Vols 1–5*, Ninth Impression (Witherby, 1943)

Eggs and nests

HARRISON C. *A Field Guide to Nests, Eggs and Nestlings of British and European Birds* (Collins, 1975)
MAYER-GROSS H. *Nest Record Scheme* (BTO Guide No. 12, 1970)

Distribution

GUEST J.P. et al *The Breeding Bird Atlas of Cheshire and Wirral* (Cheshire and Wirral Ornithological Society, 1992)
HOWARD R. & MOORE A. *A Complete Checklist of the Birds of the World* (Oxford University Press, 1980)
LACK P. ed. *The Atlas of Wintering Birds in Britain and Ireland* (Poyser, 1986)
LONG J.L. *Introduced Birds of the World: The Worldwide History, Distribution and Influence of Birds Introduced to New Environments* (David and Charles, 1981)
MALUQUER i SOSTRES Joaquim *Els Ocells de les Terres Catalanes* (Editorial Barcino, 1973)
PERCIVAL S. *Population trends in British Barn and Tawny Owls in relation to environmental change* (BTO Research Report Number 57)
SHARROCK J.T.R. *The Atlas of Breeding Birds in Britain and Ireland* (Poyser, 1976)

Names and legends connected with the barn owl

ARMSTRONG E. *The Folklore of Birds* (New Naturalist Series, 1954)
FOX-DAVIES A.G. *A Complete Guide to Heraldry* (Bloomsbury Books, 1985)
GREENOCK F. *All the Birds of the Air* (Andre Deutsch, 1979)
LOCKWOOD W.B. *The Oxford Book of British Bird Names* (Oxford University Press, 1984)

Photography

HOSKING E. *An Eye for a Bird* (Hutchinson/Arrow Books, 1973)
HOSKING E.J. and NEWBURY C.W. *Birds of the Night* (Collins, 1943)

General Index

Numbers in *italic* refer to illustrations

Index of Other Species